Bea

This is
ECSTASY

Printed and bound in the UK by MPG Books, Bodmin

Published by Sanctuary Publishing Limited, Sanctuary House,
45-53 Sinclair Road, London W14 0NS, United Kingdom

www.sanctuarypublishing.com

Photo credits in order of appearance: 1. Prof K Seddon & Dr T Evans/Queen's University, Belfast/Science Photo Library 2. Tek Image/Science Photo Library 3. Tek Image/Science Photo Library 4. James Leynes/Corbis 5. PA Photos 6. www.ecstasydata.org 7. PA Photos 8. Adrian Fisk/PYMCA 9. Tristan O'Neill/PYMCA 10. Adrian Fisk/PYMCA 11. PA Photos 12. David Swindells/PYMCA 13. Michael Tummings/PYMCA 14. Naki/PYMCA

ISBN: 1-86074-426-5

This is

ECSTASY

GARETH THOMAS

CONTENTS

INTRODUCTION

'I never had a bad time on E. I think it's great with friends. It gives you a warm feeling inside, like you can show feelings that would otherwise make you uncomfortable, and say the things that you hold back most of the time. For instance, you never tell friends how you feel about them, it's just understood – but on E you make it a point to do so. It's basically a happy pill. You're so happy, that you'd find something great in your least favorite thing. I actually cried from happiness, that's how strong it can be, but it's the happiest of cries and normally this would never ever happen because I'm simply not that emotional. A lot of this is fake of course, but after a while you can tell the difference. You can feel it throughout your body and mind. It can be smooth and subtle, or it can blow you away with its intensity. Your sense of touch is heightened enormously. Many things will feel better than normal and look better also.'

– E-mail to the author from a 24-year-old TV producer in PA, USA

'Suddenly I thought I was dying. I was screaming and all sorts. I thought I was having a heart attack and everything went black. It was horrible.'

– 'Carl', a young man quoted in the *Independent On Sunday* on 1 February 1998

This book is a treasure trove of misinformation. It's the parents' fault. Parents, bless 'em, habitually misinform as part of their brief. Both directly and subliminally through inference and body language, parents pass on outdated and just plain wrong values to their children from birth to adulthood. Their own parents, of course, misinformed them in turn. British poet Philip Larkin, reactionary misanthrope though he was, got it right when he wrote:

They fuck you up, your mum and dad
They may not mean to but they do
They fill you up with the faults they had
And add some extra just for you.

The emergence of ecstasy as the dance drug of choice has given parents, and other role models, the leeway to fuck you up like never before.

The older generations are no strangers to the drug scene. Today's parents may well have spent their own rebellious youth dropping acid to ABC, speeding to The Smiths or toking to T'Pau. Younger parents may even have formed the vanguard of the very rave culture that now corrupts their offspring. Their drugs, though, were known quantities. The dopeheads of previous generations had a fair idea of how their head was to be done in, and the likelihood of recovering afterwards.

The upstart ecstasy will have none of that. Ecstasy flips off its narcotic peers and dares to be all things to all people. The consequence is that no one really knows the slightest thing about it. Ninety years of age it *may* be, but that's just a kid in the family of narcotics. The trouble is, E is a problem child, and the modern parents can't cope with it. Parents know no more about ecstasy than do their kids, and therefore tend to acquire their knowledge via rumour and shock journalism. Their kids conversely listen to their encouraging peers' assurances, but ignore much sound scientific caution in doing so.

With this book I attempt to introduce ecstasy into polite society. It is ultimately up to each person to decide which parental messages are of value, and which have no relevance to themselves or the present time – in other words, to look to their own destiny. The book neither condones nor condemns the use of ecstasy but rather presents the latest (mis)information for young people, or their misinforming parents, to decide for themselves.

The five chapters comprise:

- **Chapter 1** – A history and overview of the rave culture. For the vast majority of participants, rave and ecstasy are the two sides of one very shiny, nay luminescent, coin. In order to understand the health, legal and political ramifications of ecstasy use, it is necessary to consider ecstasy and rave as a single entity.
- **Chapter 2** – The global manufacture and trafficking of ecstasy. This used to be a relatively benign enterprise, carried out less for profit and more for genuine comradeship. A developing worldwide competitive black market has put paid to that.
- **Chapter 3** – The history of ecstasy, with particular emphasis on its original use as an aid to psychotherapy.
- **Chapter 4** – The effect of ecstasy on short- and long-term health, explored via contradictory studies and reports that have emerged since it became a dance drug. Ecstasy is still a relatively young drug, and not much is known about it yet.
- **Chapter 5** – The media hysteria surrounding ecstasy, the legal measures that the US and UK governments have instituted because of it, and the consequent backlash by supporters of the drug.

Ecstasy is both a young drug and a drug embraced by the young. To research it I have had to enter far into the dialectal and grammatical hinterland of the 'yoof culture'. If ever there was a drug-culture equivalent to the new phenomenon of Internet chatrooms and bulletin boards, then ecstasy/rave is it. Much of my correspondence and research has come from that medium, with two particular consequences for the book.

First, the final list of recommended 'further reading' is very much an electronic one. Apart from newspapers and magazines, there is negligible printed matter on ecstasy beyond overly esoteric reports – and the only two books I list are the standard comprehensive study of the drug and the autobiography of its foremost pioneer. Most of my further reading comprises stuff that genuinely helps – websites, bulletin boards and newsgroups that present all sides of the ecstasy debate – which in turn cross-reference and offer 'further reading' matter.

Second, some of the testimonies are in the rave-culture dialect. By dialect, I mean a particular mode of language that the correspondents, many aware that they are contravening the rules of so-called 'standard' English, actively choose to use. Certainly, this is a very young and entirely printed dialect, which mainly comprises word contractions and the absence of upper-case letters and was probably brought about when thousands of youngsters suddenly wanted to communicate in real time using a keyboard, but hadn't yet mastered Mavis Beacon's Touch Typing for Windows 2000 Version 88.125. A dialect, nonetheless, it is, and in order to preserve authenticity I have usually resisted the temptation to edit these dialectic *tours de force*. Be warned.

The remarkable scientist Alexander Shulgin, who dared to nurture ecstasy when it was an infant called MDMA, had this to say – not only about ecstasy but other drugs too: 'Be informed, then choose.'

Spot on, mate.

01 CULTURE

'[We] are social, collective fucking animals and we need to be together and have a good time. It's a basic state of being alive. A basic fuckin right. These Government cunts, because they're power junkies, they are just incapable of having a good fuckin time so they want everybody else tae feel guilty, tae stay in wee boxes and devote their worthless lives tae rearing the next generation of factory fodder or sodgers or dole moles for the state. It's these boys' duty as human fuckin beings tae go oot clubbin and partying wi their friends.'

– From *Ecstasy* by Irvine Welsh

'Sire, I am from the other country. We are bored in the city, there is no longer any Temple of the Sun... And you, forgotten...without music and without geography, no longer setting out for the hacienda where the roots think of the child and where the wine is finished off with fables from an old almanac. Now that's finished. You'll never see the hacienda. It doesn't exist. The hacienda must be built.'

– from *Formula For A New Urbanism* by Ivan Chtcheglov

SPANISH HIGH

A short time ago on an island moderately far away, there was born a dance drug called ecstasy. The island was Ibiza, lying 90km (55 miles) off the east coast of Spain in the western Mediterranean, which tourist operators still describe as a place of 'peaceful countryside and secluded beaches'. Fat chance. Ibiza is, and will remain, the place where an upbeat music genre called 'house' once seduced a marriage-guidance drug called MDMA and produced 'rave' as its bastard offspring. Rave is a youth subculture comprising all-night dancing fuelled by the drug now known as ecstasy. But it is impossible to understand ecstasy without first examining the rave culture that it inspires.

OLD PLAYTIMERS

Rave is nothing new. The Ancient Greek bacchants reduce present-day ravers to abject shame by comparison. Bacchants began as mixed-gender celebrants, but in time the stronger sex took over and their parties became strictly women-only affairs. Any unfortunate male that strayed into their path would soon become legless, but not in the usual sense. In *The Sacred Mushroom And The Cross*, John M Allegro writes of the bacchants:

> *They were characterized by extreme forms of religious excitement interspersed with periods of intense depression. At one moment whirling in a frenzied dance, tossing their heads, driving one another on with screaming and the wild clamor of musical instruments, at another sunk into the deepest lethargy, and a silence so intense as to become proverbial. The Bacchants both possessed the god and were possessed by him; theirs was a religious enthusiasm in the proper sense of the term, that is, god-filled. Having eaten the Bacchus or Dionysos, they took on his power and character...*

True, the spiritual influence of the god Dionysus was really the chemical effect of *Psilocybe* mushrooms upon brain synapses; true, the bacchants' tendency to rip the limbs off human sacrifices has been honed into peace and love ideals over the millennia: but the essence of rave - drug-induced partying - was very much present and correct.

GO NATIVE

It wasn't just the definitively civilized Greeks who raved on drugs, though: orgiastic fervour has no pretensions to class or civility. Those from all parts of humankind - from the pampered sons of lords to plate-lipped Aboriginals who've never even seen cities - do, and always have, dropped drugs before dancing the night away.

The Hidatsa tribe of North Dakota, for example, used to perform the ceremony of Midhahakidutiku (Taking Up The Bowl), which symbolized the mythological 'Old Woman Who Never Dies' from Hidatsa mythology. This comprised not only drug-fuelled dancing but also the body ornamentation/mutilation that modern countercultures have claimed as their own. In *The Ceremony Of The Bowl*, Edward S Curtis writes of the Hidatsa:

> *The fasters now divided the food, and each of them took a bowl of it to one of the medicine men, a clansman of his father. When the latter had finished eating, the faster placed his hands on the medicine man's shoulders and stroked his arm to the wrists, as though receiving some power or virtue from him. His relative then sang to the spirits, imploring them to aid the faster.*
>
> *The fasters next carried food to the spectators and the medicine men, while the suppliant provided for the singers and the Keeper of the Bowl. Before eating, each one offered the food to the Four Winds and the altar. After the others had eaten and smoked, the Bowl and the suppliant and such of the fasters as chose came to the Keeper and the singers and were pierced as in the Dahpike. Slits were cut into the flesh of each breast and the inserted rawhide ropes were fastened to the cross timbers of the supporting posts of the lodge.*
>
> *The devotees in a frenzied dance made violent efforts to free themselves. Buffalo skulls were sometimes hung by thongs passed through slits in the thighs or shoulders, and other fasters were pierced through the flesh of the shoulders and suspended, their feet clear of the ground.*
>
> *The singers encouraged the dancers and kept their spirits at the highest pitch by wild singing and drumming. The fasters endured the torture as long as they were able; if they failed to tear themselves loose, or fainted with the intense pain, the Keeper of the Bowl and the singers cut the thongs and laid the exhausted dancers on their beds of sage, where they remained until the end of the ceremony, fasting and praying for visions.*

MEDIEVAL SPIRIT

It was left to Middle Ages ravers to show where dancing was really at. *The Skeptical Enquirer* of July/August 1999 writes of St Vitus' Dance:

> *A variation of tarantism [manic dancing allegedly caused by a tarantula bite] spread throughout much of Europe between the 13th and 17th centuries, where it was known as the dancing mania or St Vitus's dance, on account that participants often ended their processions in the vicinity of chapels and shrines dedicated to this saint... [Outbreaks] seized groups of people who engaged in frenzied dancing that lasted intermittently for days or weeks...These activities were typically accompanied by symptoms similar to tarantism, including screaming, hallucinations, convulsive movements, chest pains, hyperventilation, crude sexual gestures and outright intercourse. Instead of spider bites as the cause, participants usually claimed that they were possessed by demons who had induced an uncontrollable urge to dance. Like tarantism, however, music was typically played during episodes and was considered to be an effective remedy. Detailed accounts of many episodes appear in a classic book by German physician Justus Hecker,* Epidemics Of The Middle Ages *(1844). He considered the origin of these 'epidemics' as due to 'morbid sympathy', since they often coincided with periods of severe disease, such as widespread pessimism and despair after the Black Death (Hecker 1844, 87). This epic disease plague, which by some estimates killed half of the population of Europe, subsided about 20 years prior to 1374, the year that most scholars identify with the onset of the dance mania. Benjamin Gordon, in* Medieval And Renaissance Medicine *(1959, 562), describes the onset of the dance mania:*
>
> > *From Italy it spread to...Prussia, and one morning, without warning, the streets were filled... They danced together, ceaselessly, for hours or days, and in wild delirium, the dancers collapsed and fell to the ground exhausted, groaning and sighing as if in the agonies of death.*

> *When recuperated, they swathed themselves tightly with cloth around their waists and resumed their convulsive movements. They contorted their bodies, writhing, screaming and jumping in a mad frenzy. One by one they fell from exhaustion...*

Many later claimed that they had seen the walls of heaven split open and that Jesus and the Virgin Mary had appeared before them.

20TH-CENTURY WHIRL

Dropouts were more comprehensively recorded in the 20th century. During each decade or so there were separate and distinctive bands of young people, from all social classes, that stuck two fingers up at authority, then went out and got inebriated together. Uniting each class was a particular ideal, accompanied by an image, drug and music conducive to it. Here's a list.

1910s/1920s
BOHEMIANS

- Identity: artists, writers, workers, anarchists and socialists would debate art, writing work, anarchism and socialism; and drink in cafés.
- Drug(s) of choice: coffee, absinthe.
- Musical influences: Debussy, Ravel, Rachmaninov.

1930s
WEST END JAZZ FIENDS

- Identity: idle rich folk would congregate in London's West End, get high and listen to the latest swing sound in clubs.
- Drug(s) of choice: cocaine.
- Musical influences: Louis Armstrong's Hot Five, Cab Calloway And His Orchestra, Bix Beiderbecke And His Gang.

1940s
CONSCIENTIOUS OBJECTORS

- Identity: left-leaning poets would exchange quatrains and hand jobs; and sit out World War II.

- Drug(s) of choice: spirits, tobacco.
- Musical influences: Benjamin Britten, Michael Tippett.

1950s

BEATNIKS

- Identity: pretentious young people would hang out in retreats, debate existentialism, revere Ginsberg and snigger about the dildo in Burroughs' *Naked Lunch*.
- Drug(s) of choice: marijuana.
- Musical influences: Charles Mingus, John Coltrane, Thelonious Monk.

1960s

MODS AND ROCKERS

- Identity: cool dudes on Harleys would line up against wusses on scooters and reduce the natives of Brighton to collective apoplexy.
- Drug(s) of choice: alcohol, speed.
- Musical influences: Rolling Stones, The Who, Small Faces.

HIPPIES

- Identity: spiritual young folk would paint their faces, wear flowers in their hair and avoid such luxuries as soap and shampoo.
- Drug(s) of choice: hashish, LSD.
- Musical influences: Jefferson Airplane, The Grateful Dead, later Beatles.

1970s

PUNKS

- Identity: middle-class youths would dress down, attend concerts and spit at the band.
- Drug(s) of choice: alcohol, speed, poppers.
- Musical influences: The Sex Pistols, The Damned, The Clash, The Buzzcocks.

1980s

ACID HOUSERS

- Identity: Rebellious teenagers would break into warehouses, drop tabs and occasionally jump from upstairs windows whilst flapping their arms.

- Drug(s) of choice: LSD.
- Musical influences: Happy Mondays, M/A/R/R/S, Jim Silk, Black Box.

MEDIA MUDDIES

I've just stereotyped a century's worth of youth cultures, and I'm about to do it again. Blame the media. The rave culture - and therefore, by association, the ecstasy culture - is but the latest in this line of dropout fads originated by genuine young people with a message, but named and therefore given identity by the populist and media press of the time.

The media loves a good subculture. The more depraved the subculture - the more faces are slashed and brains are fried - the better it is, and the more the media loves it. To ensure a constant supply of subcultures, the tabloid press and populist TV documentaries help them develop beyond their putative stage: they root out a localized craze and mass publicize it to a national epidemic. Had Elvis not gyrated his pelvis (before the magic of hamburgers made his trademark body part too deep-set for him to see, let alone gyrate), the audience seats at the *Ed Sullivan Show* would have remained dry from teenage girls; had the Stones not been caught pissing on a garage wall, they may still be remembered as 'that band that might have done all right if they'd ditched the ugly rubber-lipped bloke'; had the Pistols not been goaded to call Bill Grundy a 'dirty fucker' on early-evening television, Sid might never have met Nancy and still be alive and managing a pub; had the Beastie Boys not shared the stage with caged go-go dancers and a 1.5m (5ft) hydraulic penis, Volkswagen logos would never have been pulled from Passats for use as pendants.

YOU SCRATCH MY HACK

The media and subcultures feed upon each other. The populist tabloids of necessity instil excitement into the humdrum existences of readers by offering more titillating matter than budget predictions or the DOW index. Nothing titillates better than a feeling of superiority, and a nice scare story about current youth fads makes the residents of Middle England and the

US Bible Belt feel very superior indeed. Things need names to exist, so the media has to apply labels to fads: most likely different ones than the faddists would have devised. The terms 'acid house' and 'rave' are inventions of the media.

In an e-mail to the author, one US raver spells out his frustration at such crass categorization (I use the word 'spells' in its loosest possible sense): 'This is a big generalization. There no specific style for party kids or ravers. But most party kids listen to HOUSE and where phat pants and sweatshirts. Other than raver's most people I know that use e don't really have a specific style. See, people generalize drug user's to much. You need to realize each kid is different. Just because they use a certain drug doesn't mean they automatically conform to a style that goes with that drug. C'mon now that just doesn't make any sense. I mean we're not in junior high anyomore. Well, most of us, anyway.'

BARD TALK

The absurdity of genre classification has been recognized since Shakespeare's time. Polonius tells Hamlet about it prior to the Elsinore Castle 'let's freak out Claudius' gig. Of the travelling players, he says:

> *The best actors in the world, either for tragedy, comedy, history, pastoral, pastoral-comical, historical-pastoral, tragical-historical, tragical-comical-historical-pastoral, scene individable, or poem unlimited: Seneca cannot be too heavy nor Plautus too light. For the law of writ and the liberty, these are the only men.*
>
> – From *Hamlet*, Act II, Scene ii

If there exists such a thing as 'genre', it is only as a term of the greatest convenience. Different works within the same category are often, like Lech Walesa and General Jaruzelski, poles apart. Historical genre dichotomies include:

- Byron's 'Don Juan' vs Keats' 'On Melancholy' – extrovert satire vs introvert self-pity;

- Beethoven's *Eroica Symphony* vs Schubert's *Winterreise* - public egalitarianism vs intimate individualism;
- Brooke's 'The Old Vicarage, Grantchester' vs Owen's 'Anthem For Doomed Youth' - sentimental patriotism vs war-scarred anger;
- Louis Armstrong's 'What A Wonderful World' vs Dave Brubeck's 'Take Five' - schmaltz vs rhythm;
- The Beatles' *Abbey Road* vs The Rolling Stones' *Beggar's Banquet* - flower power vs white blues;
- The Sex Pistols' 'Anarchy In The UK' vs Damned's 'New Rose' - UK nihilism vs US-style garage.

It follows that the remainder of this chapter is, in the words of my American friend, a 'big generalization'. It's both simplistic and stereotypical. It's true enough, though.

HISTORY OF RAVE

THE ROCK 'N' ROLL (AND DISCO) YEARS

There is no abrupt change between youth movements: John Lennon did not wake up one sunny late 1960s morning, see trees of green and skies of blue, and think to himself, 'What a wonderful day to begin flower power'; Malcolm McLaren did not write 'invent British punk' into his long-term diary for 1976.

Rather, there is an overlap, with one movement gradually dying out while another gains ascendancy. They segue into each other. In a sense differentiation between one subculture and one that precedes or follows it (or is contemporary) is a generalization. The later 1960s didn't hang up their anthropomorphic roller-skates and just cease to swing, in favour of wearing a poncho and toking at three-day festivals. For sure, acts like Crosby, Stills and Nash, Joan Baez and Jefferson Airplane fostered their decadent lovemaking ways upon upstanding American patriots; but non-hippie bands like The Who, the MC5 and the

The risks of consuming LSD and ecstasy are increased enormously by their illegal and unsupervised manufacture. Ecstasy consumption was down 13 per cent in 2001, despite prices falling to £4.12 ($5.97) a pill, compared to £8.83 ($12.80) in 1999.

Stooges were all going strong alongside them. Even Sha-na-na played at Woodstock alongside the deadbeats.

A teenager would not have woken up one 1977 morning and found that punk rock had reared its spiked head above the phlegm-thick surface and dispatched glam rock, progressive rock and disco to a kitsch hinterland. Far from it: a typical edition of that year's *Old Grey Whistle Test* (a UK music show that featured live acts in a studio setting) would feature such diverse acts as Queen, ELP and – yes – punk outfit X-Ray Spex.

Likewise the house, acid house and rave movements of the late 1980s and early 1990s by no means dispatched post-punk (as well as anodyne ballads like Bryan Adams' 'Everything I Do' and Nik Kershaw's 'I Won't Let the Sun Go Down on Me) to the kitsch hinterland alongside the flared 1970s crew. Indeed, house's roots as a medium for live disc jockeys meant that those tracks that did find their heavy-beated way to the popular music charts were within themselves oxymorons, because they clocked in at scandalously short play-times like seven minutes; and actually started and finished.

Although house, acid house and rave did after a fashion follow on the spit-drenched tails of the post-punk movement, they didn't kick it from the limelight. Far from it – it only seems that way from reading retrospective music histories. Different styles continued side by side; indeed post-punk is an essential movement to consider if one is to witness the rave phenomenon in context.

POST RIPPED

Post-punk bands encompassed such diverse sounds as the retro-glam-rock posturing of Duran Duran and Adam And The Ants; the life-affirming ska of Madness and The Specials; the comedy punk of The Undertones and The Toy Dolls; the gloomy ambience of Magazine and Bauhaus; the angst of the later Buzzcocks and The Smiths and the avant-garde noise of Sonic Youth and Wire. Although sounding drastically different from one another, these groups retained punk's aggression but either rejected the out-and-out nihilism of bands like The Sex Pistols and The Dead Kennedys or expressed it more poetically. Most significant were those bands – like Wire, Echo And The Bunnymen, Sonic Youth and the post-1970s Damned (who adapted to each new musical trend with some success) – that rejected punk's simple riffs in favour of 'artistic' experimentation, and in doing so almost referenced the progressive-rock genre that punk had tried to discredit. For example, The Damned's 1980 song 'Curtain Call', far from being a three-minute garage song, clocks in at over 17 minutes, and includes violin cadenzas from 19th-century Russian composer Rimsky-Korsakov's *Arabian Nights*-inspired *Sheherazade*. Sonic Youth had the temerity to release, in 1988, a double album called *Daydream Nation* that, far from encapsulating the three-minute pop song, ended with a 20-minute 'Trilogy'. That's the sort of thing those tedious progressive rockers did.

Post-punk appealed to students, former prog-rockers and sophisticates, who retrospectively accepted the original punk bands as the acceptable forerunners of their 'scene'. Post-punk therefore became the established 'arty-farty' scene that house attempted to subvert, in the same way that punk's first wave had threatened progressive rock. House didn't succeed, as the 1990s mainstream successes of bands like Nirvana, Pearl Jam and Garbage would testify, but it did crucially revive a music scene that was starting to stagnate.

FULL CONTRAPUNTAL ASSAULT

New trends emerged in counterpoint to post-punk. The soul and funk that dominated 1970s discos increasingly developed the synthesizer-based electronic sound pioneered by Giorgio Moroder on Donna Summer's 'I Feel Love'. Simultaneously, the High Energy (Hi-NRG) movement invaded US gay clubs: this was an upbeat sound characterized by speeded-up dance cuts and strong melody lines typified by songs like Aimi Stewart's 'Knock On Wood' and Patrick Hernandez's 'Born To Be Alive'. Other typical artists included Divine (a transvestite, but not the shit-munching near-namesake from the underground John Waters film *Pink Flamingos*) and the Canadians Gino Soccio and France Joli.

Bobby Orlando, also known as Bobby O, a seminal Hi-NRG songwriter and producer, said that the purpose of the Hi-NRG scene was 'to feel good and positive'. Not a world of difference from the ethic of a later ecstasy-fuelled dance movement...

THE GOSPEL YOUTH

Meanwhile in New York labels like Sal Soul introduced remixes and versions of inherently upbeat gospel songs; while in the UK, genres like hip-hop and individual songs like Lipps Inc's 'Funkytown' made their dubious presence known in nightclubs and discotheques. These were joined by edgier disco records from the US underground scene like D Train's 'You're The One for Me' and The Peech Boys' 'Don't Make Me Wait', which introduced dub and dropouts to the existing drum track.

NEW ORDER

At the time that post-punk reached its apex and finest moment with The Smiths' 1986 album *The Queen Is Dead*, another Manchester band, New Order, were developing their definitive sound, culminating in their magnum opus *Technique* in 1989. This superlative record - the first great album of the rave era - is the antithesis of the band's early output. Indeed the ten-year transition between their two albums *Unknown Pleasures* and *Technique* exactly mirrors the changeover from post-punk to rave.

Starting as a typically substandard punk combo called Warsaw, the band had the foresight to hire a professional record producer, Martin Hannett, who forged them into the unique outfit Joy Division. Purveyors of the most downbeat Gothic gloom imaginable, Joy Division's frontman Ian Curtis sang lyrics with enigmatic meaning but clear subtexts of rejection, isolation and suicide. Their two studio albums *Unknown Pleasures* and *Closer*, as well as individual tracks like 'Shadowplay' and 'Atrocity Exhibition', are dark masterpieces (though I wouldn't sit in the passenger seat beside someone who still listens to them).

❤ IS GETTING YOUR FACTS RIGHT

The BBC websites gathered under a retro umbrella called 'I ❤' - that includes varying spokes of psychedelic colour, kitsch mock-tartan and Gothic black - are an invaluable source of knowledge on cultural trends. Pedants who watched the UK television shows that bred the sites, and who noted the frequent abominable inaccuracy of the research (the Rubik's Cube craze being attributed to 1979 and the Space Invaders one to 1985 are prime examples) can rest assured that these sites are far more authoritative. There is no need for these latterday *Simpsons* comic-book guys to deluge Internet bulletin boards with their sarcastic comments.

The 'I ❤ Manchester' site (whether or not you agree with the sentiment) offers helpful information about the UK rave scene and its musical roots. Of Joy Division, it says:

> *Originally called Warsaw, Joy Division took their name from the prostitution wing of a concentration camp, and emerged in 1978 as one of the most important groups of their era. After recording a regionally available EP, 'An Ideal For Living', they were signed to the recently formed Factory Records.*
>
> *Basing their sound in Peter Hook's bass and Stephen Morris's drums, the band released two albums, the stark and insistent* Unknown Pleasures *and the emotional and brilliant* Closer. *The songs they produced were critically acclaimed, if relatively unsuccessful commercially.*
>
> *Their live performances were electric, entrancing affairs, led by the jerky, neurotic dancing of lead singer Ian Curtis. Tragically, Ian suffered from epilepsy, the condition and treatment of which would lead to his suicide at the age of 23.*

After 18 May 1980, when Curtis practised what he preached with the aid of a well-tied noose and an Iggy Pop record, the band began its nine-year fashioning of the UK rave sound.

The band's first post-Curtis album, *Movement*, was basically 'Joy Division Lite', but replacing Curtis with the drummer's girlfriend (Gillian Gilbert) and making the quietly spoken but amiable guitarist Bernard Albrecht the singer (under his real and less Germanic name of Bernard Sumner) put paid to that. New Order's mature voice was upbeat and electronic, and their lyrics entirely trite. Each successive album *Power, Corruption And Lies*, *Low Life* and *Brotherhood*, as well as singles like 'Blue Monday' and 'True Faith', moved more toward the definitive rave sound pioneered by *Technique* – a record so redolent of Ibiza that you can taste the paella.

'I ❤ Manchester' gives this hyperbolic account of the band (they weren't/aren't quite that good):

> *Manchester must always be grateful for one thing – that Stephen Morris, Bernard Sumner and Peter Hook liked the music biz enough not to jack it all in when Ian Curtis took his own life, for without New Order, the sound of this fair city could have been very different.*
>
> *Moving Bernard onto vocals and recruiting Stephen's then-girlfriend, now missus, Gillian Gilbert to take on keyboard and guitar duties, New Order took over the mighty mantle Joy Division had left behind and spent the '80s and early '90s defining the listening lives of a generation.*
>
> *The achievements speak for themselves. Six critically acclaimed and commercially successful albums between 1981 and 1993 (*Movement, Power, Corruption And Lies, Low Life, Brotherhood, Technique *and* Republic*), the biggest-selling 12" of all time (the mighty 'Blue Monday'), a myriad of genius singles including 'Ceremony', 'Shellshock', 'True Faith', 'The Perfect Kiss', 'Touched By The Hand Of God', 'Fine Time', 'Run 2', 'Bizarre Love Triangle' and 'Regret', and probably the best football song ever written in 'World In Motion'.*
>
> *Then came a break for solo projects and many rumours about splits, arguments and the end of the group. Peter formed Revenge and later Monaco, Bernard teamed up with ex-Smiths guitarist and Manchester legend Johnny Marr to form Electronic, and Gillian and Stephen produced tracks as The Other Two.*
>
> *Thankfully, though, the rumours were wrong, the band did come back together and* Get Ready *[New Order's critically acclaimed 2001 comeback album] followed* Republic *after an eight-year gap, and the single 'Crystal' made us all believe they never went away.*

New Order's development reflected the general trend of the 1980s. Post-punk, New Romantic and Goth bands like Echo and the Bunnymen, the Teardrop Explodes, the Cure and the Mission were gradually accompanied in the charts by the electronic music of Kraftwerk, Depeche Mode and New Order; and by the faster and happier music from the likes of T'Pau and the Communards.

They were soon joined in the charts and (especially) nightclubs by a seminal sound from the States: house music. More on that later.

TRITE SUPREMACY

Punk's less street-cred partner in crime, disco, was in the sorriest of states at this time. Although gobbed at both figuratively and literally by the punk movement, disco had slogged it out for ten years and – while the 1970s stereotype of white men with Afros, bell-bottoms, and shirts that were even louder than the music, did its image no good at all – it had produced genuinely fine numbers like Sister Sledge's 'He's the Greatest Dancer' and Odyssey's 'Native New Yorker'. It didn't last. During the 1980s, disco reached its butt-end and coughed up phlegm and catarrh in the form of musical atrocities like Ottawan's 'DISCO'.

A more reprehensible aspect of disco music than just sheer bad taste was its tacit acceptance of racist attitudes. After white artists first appreciated black music – with the spirituals and rags of the late 19th century – they appropriated and, by implication, 'refined' it. The inference was that black people, and therefore their music, were somehow more primitive and 'inferior to' whites. This attitude hit its perversely ironic nadir with the UK skinheads of the 1970s, who would work themselves into a frenzy with reggae music while suggesting with a select application of the Doctor Marten boot that originators of said music might like to reside elsewhere. In other words, Commonwealth citizens should return to those countries the British Empire stole from them the previous century.

In *Cultural Hegemony In Music: A 'Struggle' Of The Privileged*, AS Van Dorston writes of this trend (I have abridged this):

> *The continued influence of the racist attitude can be traced to the rock 'n' roll music industry. Ever since whites first recognized African-American folk music as real music, it has been 'borrowed' in order to facilitate the success of white performers like the Christy Minstrels*

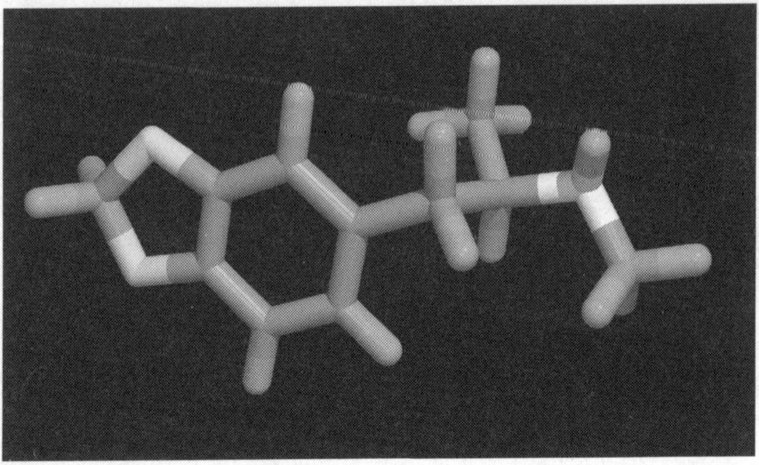

Computer artwork of a molecule of the drug ecstasy (3,4-methylenedioxymethampetamine, or MDMA [formula $C_{11}H_{14}NO_2$]). The atoms are shown as cylinders.

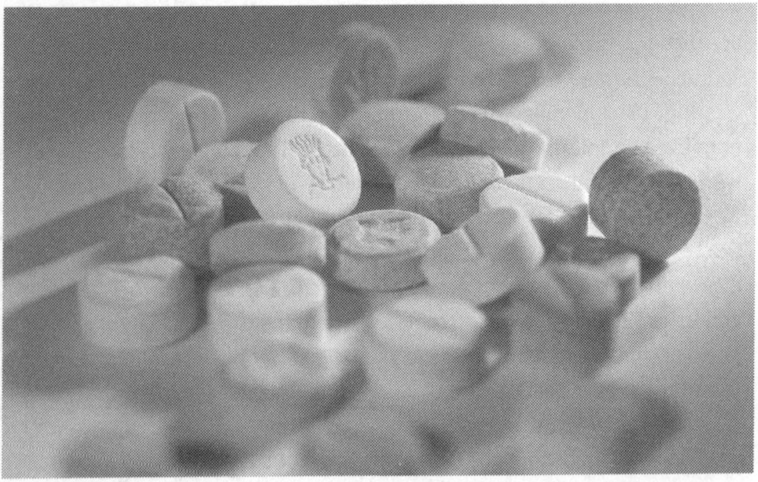

Ecstasy is one of the numerous so-called 'designer drugs' that originated in the USA in the mid-1980s, and the pills come in many different sizes and shapes. Designer drugs are made illicitly by chemists who may alter the structures of existing compounds (which may have been legislated against) to create a chemically different substance that retains the active properties of the original. Alterations to a large and complex molecule to adjust its legal status yet retain potency could be relatively easy for an experienced chemist – often the substitution of hydrogen for a fluorine atom may be sufficient.

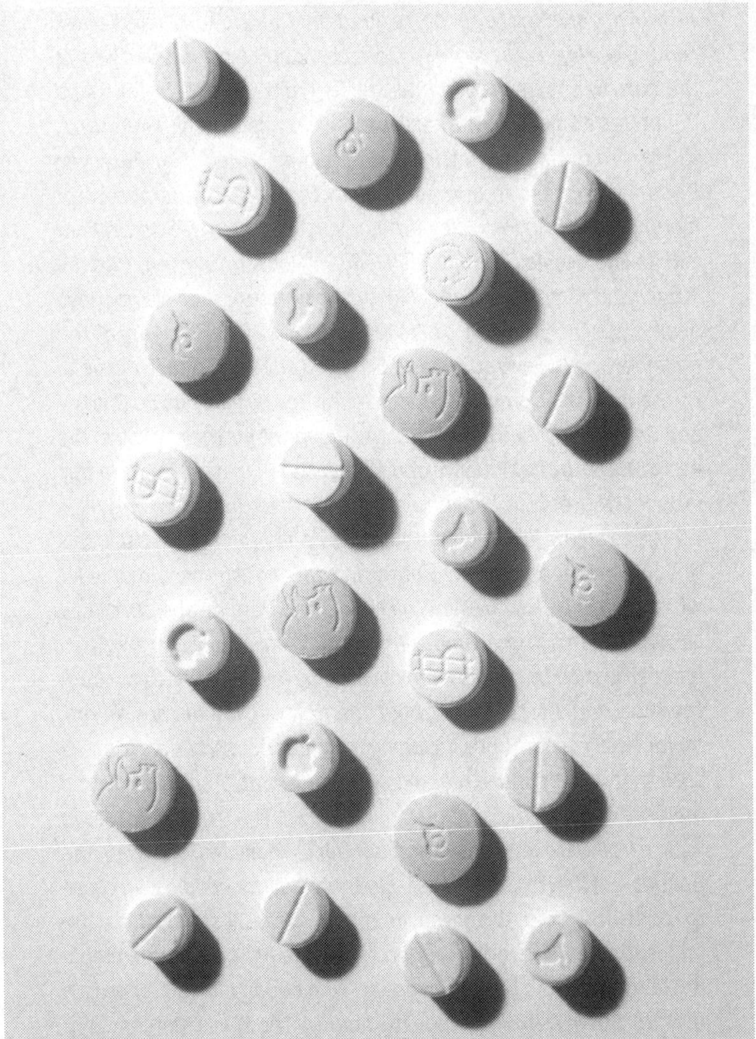

Ecstasy is an illegal drug that gives users a sense of well-being, affection for the people around them and increased energy. Possible short-term problems associated with its use include feeling ill, a sense of losing control, and dehydration, while long-term problems include loss of memory and weight. The deaths associated with the use of ecstasy are generally caused by an accumulation of water in the brain due to the way in which the drug affects the body's internal signals rather than directly due to the drug's toxicity.

with black skin makeup, or 'refined' by European-trained black composers like Louis Moreau Gottschalk and Edmond Dede to fit the narrow spectrum of white music. From Duke Ellington's and Count Basie's swing to the black pioneers of ragtime, blues and jazz, the record businesses owned by white men stifled their deserved financial success in comparison to the white benefactors of manufactured Tin Pan Alley tunes. Even by the late 1930s, brilliant artists like Bessie Smith, Billie Holiday, Robert Johnson, Big Joe Turner and Tampa Red were unknown to everyone who did not have access to the handful of 'race' record stores in segregated neighborhoods. Few radio stations played any sort of 'race music.'... By the time Fats Domino, BB King, Sonny Boy Williamson, Bo Diddley and Chuck Berry had developed the blueprint for rock 'n' roll in the early 1950s, the baby-boom generation began to grow into a highly influential group of consumers, giving the industry incentive to capitalize on the junk teenage culture and abandon any elitist ideals of sophistication in music. But at first the industry would only let white men like Elvis Presley, Bill Haley, Carl Perkins and Jerry Lee Lewis become rich and famous from rock 'n' roll. Many songs written and performed by blacks were covered by faceless whites that put them on the charts. Throughout the first decade of rock 'n' roll, major label corporations including RCA, Capitol and Atlantic made sure that white culture reigned supreme, if only in illusion, with a majority of performers plagiarizing blacks... The true celebrities in rock 'n' roll were always white, from Buddy Holly to Bob Dylan, the Beatles and the Rolling Stones... Meanwhile, black people who chose to continue bold progress in music were restricted to the underground. With the exception of Jimi Hendrix, a prime example is George Clinton's band Funkadelic, who began making records in the late '60s in Detroit, by then the home of the Black Panther Party. They synthesized a brilliant hybrid of soul, R&B, rock 'n' roll and funk, with cocky lyrics inspired by the radicalism of black politics in Detroit. Because they represented the very same kind of class wars that the expositions at the turn of the century aimed to squash,

Funkadelic and their small label were completely ignored by the music industry, and despite their inspired influence in music, banned from the rock 'n' roll press and history books... By the 1970s corporate FM radio had taken possession of the airwaves, further segregating blacks from the cultural hegemony of rock 'n' roll. While black music managed to maintain artistic progress with the British skinhead support of soul, ska, reggae, and the rich integration of the 2-tone movement. [Maybe skinheads supported the music but – with notable exceptions like the bands Sham 69 and The Angelic Upstarts – they actively persecuted the people that made it.] America only had disco. Disco provided only an extremely limited form of commercial artistic exposure for a few black musicians. It was often viewed as an inferior form of music, as embarrassing as African-American folk music was to white people at the turn of the century.

NEW HOUSE

Disco had become an embarrassment with racist undertones, so it's just as well – for its reputation's sake – that it bred house music.

Ravers worldwide should tip their hats to Chicago, for it was the Windy City that both created and named house music. In the disco era it was Chicago that forged the electronic drum track and pioneered the 12" 45rpm EP (Extended Play) record intended specifically for disc jockeys. These, though, were inconsequential compared to Chicago's greatest attribute. Chicago had an asset that was absolutely fundamental to the creation of house – a nightclub called the Warehouse.

WAREHOUSE ROCK

It was not until the Warehouse opened in 1977 that Chicago became remotely a dance city. Until then Chicago was known as the home of the greatest blues acts around and was home or host to such iconic figures as John Lee Hooker, Howlin' Wolf, Muddy Waters, Elmore James and Willie Dixon. Chicago dance clubs, in as much as they existed, used jukeboxes rather than live disc jockeys and, in common with the rest of the US, tended to segregate different races and sexual preferences into their own distinct clubs.

When disco hit its apex in 1977, a successful New York disc jockey, Frankie Knuckles (not to be confused with his skeletal near-namesake Frankie Bones, whose time would come later), noticed the Windy City's live-music vacuum and determined to fill it by opening The Warehouse, which was revolutionary in two main senses (other than that involving discs and turntables).

First, it ditched the racism. The Warehouse welcomed people from across the race (and sexual preference) barriers, and played an eclectic mix of musical styles. Knuckles alternated the disparate genres R&B (rhythm and blues), disco and punk, with results that were beneficial to all three. He writes: 'When we first opened in 1977, I was playing a lot of the east Coast records, the Philly stuff, Salsoul. By '80/81, when that stuff was all over with, I started working a lot of the soul that was coming out. I had to re-construct the records to work for my dancefloor, to keep the dancefloor happy, as there was no dance music coming out! I'd take the existing songs, change the tempo, layer different bits of percussion over them, to make them more conducive for the dancefloor.'

By 1981, Knuckles had built the prototype of the house sound by remaking and remixing records with added percussion tracks live in the club – in effect becoming a live musical performer. He would perform such spinning salaciousness as playing a Roland 909 drum machine under old Soyl records – thus emphasizing the beats or mixing in rhythm tracks from reel-to-reel tape recorders.

Second, its name was shortened to 'house'. What a useful name for a new music genre...

RADIO RAVES

Other DJs and music-industry figures joined the house bandwagon and contributed to the new hybrid sound. One outlet for the trend was Chicago's WBMX radio station – which featured such DJs as Farley 'Jackmaster' Funk (who later hosted dances at a rival Chicago club called The Playground) and Ralphie Rosario.

House music started off as familiar disco music given a persistent and pounding beat; this rhythm becoming of far more significance than any odd lyrics that might wind their way coherently to dancers' ears. Gradually other DJs, courtesy of Knuckles' example, realised the live-performance potential of their job and began the unofficial game of 'Who can mix the weirdest sound into a classic soul track?'

BIG PIONEERS

House music was not initially assigned to vinyl but recorded on cassette tape for exclusive use in clubs, and opinion is divided as to which was the first house record released, though it was probably an obscure track called 'Fantasy' by Z Factor.

Some disagree and attribute the first commercial house record to Jesse Saunders, who was resident disc jockey at The Playground around 1983. The story goes that some rapscallion with rhythm made off with Saunders' favourite dance mix, so the DJ had to remake it himself using his own equipment. He then thought, 'What the hell? Might as well try and flog this for my troubles', and released the 1983 single 'Fantasy', which was followed later the same year by 'On and On'. Mixed into this track were arcade game sounds, songs by Donna Summer, and Lipps Inc's atrocious 'Funkytown'.

Chicago DJ Steve Hurley was another vinyl house pioneer: his seminal release 'Music is the Key' spurred the formation of record label DJ International which, along with Larry Sherman's Trax Records, dominated the house market in its early years.

Artists developing the house sound during this time included Chip E, whose song 'Like This' introduced the sampled stutter technique that is now as big a part of rave as baggy trousers and body odour.

DUB IT YOURSELF

In 1986 disc jockey Marshall Jefferson earned his anointment as 'King of House' by synthesizing the 'deep house' sound that was to become the quintessential club vibe. Meanwhile gay disc jockey Ron Hardy was dabbling with dark forces in the form of raw and wild rhythm tracks that made Jefferson's sound seem like Flanders and Swann's 'The Hippopotamus Song' in comparison. Hardy's club The Music Box introduced singers of the calibre of Liz Torres and Keith Nonally to the dancing public's ear, though it was another of Hardy's innovations that had the greatest long-term effect on house: he held open forums for aspiring disc jockeys, inviting newcomers to test their home-grown compilation tapes on a live audience. As with British punk of the 1970s, this 'do it yourself' approach reaped phenomenal benefits for the spread of the genre.

BODY ART

The two primary house hits of 1996 held titles that might be said by an aerobics instructor: Eiffel 65's 'Move Your Body' was the original 'house anthem', while Jim Silk's 'Jack Your Body' (actually January 1997) achieved the feat of transforming a paucity of lyrics and a stuttering 'J' sound into something approaching iconic. Such profundity earned it the honour of being the first house number to top the UK pop charts.

However it was the 'Jack'-less 'Move Your Body' that initially catapulted house music into the UK. The song was a mainstay of pirate radio stations like disc jockey Jazzy M's London Weekend Radio (LWR), and other songs in the oeuvre soon followed. Meanwhile London's Delirium Club became the first UK nightclub dedicated to the house sound. Soon, a combo ever-so-wittily called the Chicago House Party toured the UK; and included Marshall Jefferson himself amongst its array of disc jockeys.

BAD GIGS

There may an element of rose-tinted-specs-wearing in reminiscences of early ravers. A correspondent gives this account of the early rave scene, which suggests that events could be anything but eight-hour manifestations of unity and respect: 'I sadly can't say that I was there in the very beginning. Clubbers who witnessed those select gatherings in dodgy warehouses or parties on the beach in Ibiza still reminisce like war veterans, almost wearing their "smiley" badges like campaign medals. Although aware of the growing scene through friends I passed on it as they tended to be more into speed and "animal" (their nickname for amyl nitrate). Although I attended a rave they had organized (called "Jellyhead") back at the end of the '80s, it was more notable for some local violent score settling than any loved-up euphoria. The hard-house menacing energy reminded more of local village-hall punk gigs from a decade before. A mate of mine describes – with unusual honesty – how crap he remembered the early free party scene was. He recalls cruising endlessly round the M25 until the mobile call came in, arriving in a field only half an hour before the police shut everything down, and then getting back into a car full of people grinding their teeth and babbling like hardened speed freaks. I stuck to beer and hash.'

LANCASHIRE HOT SPOT

It was 300km (200 miles) northwest in Manchester that house music really took off in the UK. In particular the legendary Hacienda club, with its disc jockey Mike Pickering, devoted whole nights to house music, and would later become synonymous with the UK rave scene.

THE HACIENDA MUST BE BUILT

It's appropriate that the manager of New Order started it all off. The Hacienda was the direct descendent of Manchester's punk venue the Factory club, run by Tony Wilson, who also owned the Factory record label on which Joy Division/New Order released their records. When the Factory club closed in 1981, Wilson along with Joy Division manager Rob Gretton planned to replace it with a purpose-built club to rival New York venues like the Danceteria, Fun House and Paradise Garage. Funded by New Order, Factory and Whitbread (a brewery), the new club was designed by Ben Kelly within the deserted International Marine Centre.

MDMA (methylenedioxymethamphetamine) was first synthesized and then patented some time before 1912 by the German pharmaceutical giant Merck, as part of a search to create a new 'styptic' medication that stops bleeding.

The Hacienda, named after a passage from the 1953 Situationalist text *Formula For A New Urbanism*, was opened by Bernard Manning, of all people (see p138 for more on this rotund racist), on 21 May 1982, with Hewan Clark as the disc jockey. Clark would return the following night – and every subsequent one for the next four years.

With commendable continuity Factory allotted the Hacienda a 'catalogue number', as it had with its record releases. The Hacienda was 'Factory Product 51'. The Hacienda was a multi-levelled affair, with a dancefloor, galleries, a basement and ornaments that included road bollards to prevent girls' high heels getting stuck in grooves at the dancefloor's edge. It adopted a multicultural approach akin to that used by Frankie Knuckles at the Warehouse. It wasn't a house venue at first: typical pre-house artists included Erasure, the Jesus and Mary Chain and, topping the bill, *Coronation Street*'s Vera Duckworth, singing a medley of her favourite songs.

That all changed when the Chicago House Party visited the club in 1987, and the new genre took precedence. Music journalist John McCready says of the first impressions of house:

> *House certainly sounded new back then (obviously we weren't as clever as we are now in spotting the disco roots of the sound), but it was still polite. Acid was a different sound altogether – menacing, growling, ungrateful and volatile, at its best like a starved dog prowling in circles. But acid sounded like coded radio signals, a kind of dance instruction from another planet.*
>
> – From *Working On A Building Of Love*

THE HACIENDA MUST BE CLOSED

Twelve years later, following the 1992 crash of Factory Records and subsequent incidents of violence and drug dealing, the Hacienda closed down. The Urban75 Rave website gives this account of the iconic venue's final rave-cum-squat in June 1999:

> *The thousand or so party-goers inside were matched by almost as many again outside, as police moved in at midnight to prevent any more people from gaining entrance to the building, squatted since the previous day. When their cheeky attempt at storming the building was repelled by vigilant party people, the cops went wild outside, randomly batonning anyone who seemed most lively. One particularly excited six and a half foot [2m] uniformed officer struck*

> *someone straight across the back, before this plain clothes guy cried out, 'I'm a copper, you idiot!'*
>
> *The sound system eventually was negotiated out at 8am. Until then overhead, the police helicopter spotlight swept over determined party-heads getting hauled up into windows or shuffling along ledges, and all those still circling the building.*

FIRST WAVE OF RAVE

In 1987 the first in a succession of tabloid scares dropped through the letterboxes of bigots and ignoramuses. Young, clearly demented people were breaking into warehouses, playing loud music and dropping tabs of LSD. This depravity was traced to the Spanish island of Ibiza, formerly a favourite resort where retired Britons would stretch their bony legs, but now a veritable vice den; a throwback to the days when various invaders would try and make the island their own, though the earlier ones were less subtle, using battleaxes rather than beatboxes as their mode of persuasion. The *Daily Mail*, a reactionary British tabloid, wrote at the time:

> *The drugs culture took a disturbing new turn at the weekend when the biggest ever 'acid house' party was held... As 11,000 youngsters descended on a quiet airfield in the middle of the night, drug pushers were waiting to tempt them with an evil selection of narcotics.*

Despite the shock journalism, this was low-key stuff – low-key, that is, until the media distorted it into something endemic, and set about a self-fulfilling prophesy by calling the trend 'acid house'. At first it just consisted of two unrelated groups throwing all-night dance parties. Psychic TV, fronted by the redoubtable Genesis P Orridge, had a hardcore edge – but enough about them, for the ones that mattered were Schoom, because they partied to the newfangled music called house.

Acid house was to UK farmers of the late 1980s what foot-and-mouth disease is to them now: it took over their holdings and made them uninhabitable until the pestilence was cleared. Bizarre young people wearing smiley-face T-shirts would occupy their fields all night long, playing music and shouting, 'Acieeeeed!' in high-pitched voices. What the media dubbed the 1988 Summer of Love had begun. So had rave.

Meanwhile, in Germany, Berlin bigots were bearing the same paranoiac burden as their British brothers in bigotry, and for the same reason: young Deutschers were breaking into warehouses, too. Curiously, the Berlin rave culture exactly mirrored that of the UK – including its rapid commercialization.

Back in Britain, after farmers had sent a combination of the law, shotgun pellets and rutting bulls after the trespassing partiers, they were forced to seek out alternative venues with at least some chance of covert activity.

In 1989–90, the British Government responded to the Middle England hysteria by introducing new laws to shut down the raves. Following the mandatory abandonment of warehouses – once the constabulary had visited and declined to embrace either the ravers' love-and-peace ideals or the ravers themselves – the all-night parties relocated to Manchester, sparking what 'hilariously' became known as the Madchester scene, which focused on the aforementioned Hacienda club.

IT'S VIM UP NORTH

Manchester never used to have the sunniest of images. The opening titles of *Coronation Street*, the music of Joy Division and The Smiths, stock footage of pissing-down rain on terraced houses – that was the 'Manchester scene' prior to the late 1980s. Then Joy Division became New Order, the International Marine Centre became the Hacienda and The Stone Roses became the new Beatles, Rolling Stones and Sex Pistols combined. Manchester became Madchester, the UK focus for the rave scene where students, pseudo-hippies and proto-new-agers would converge to dance, drop E and occasionally collapse from dehydration. The overall mood was that of a unity and optimism that the UK hadn't felt as a subculture since the hippie days of the 1960s.

The familiar musical London versus Manchester rivalry now decidedly favoured the mop-haired northerners, with three bands in particular – The Stone Roses, Happy Mondays and The Inspiral Carpets – leading the nationwide music scene. It was the first of these bands that as good as proclaimed themselves the 'messiahs of Madchester', with their song 'I Am The Resurrection'. They more or less got away with this Mancunian messianic posturing until their turgid follow-up album *Second Coming* revealed their real status as less the 'new Beatles' than the new 'Emerson, Lake And Palmer meet Led Zeppelin'. Nonetheless, during the Madchester years, they defined the times – cocky, optimistic and anti-materialistic.

LONDON FOLLOWING

Inevitably England's capital muscled in on the act and the rave scene spread to the clubs and open areas of London. In March 1990 the Criminal Justice March took place in Trafalgar Square, beginning with the UK's best riot in years and culminating with 'Biology', its biggest ever illegal party. This assured London's place as a rave city, and house/techno became pretty well ubiquitous in its clubs. Venues such as Club UK and the Ministry of Sound, became prime rave venues during the early to mid-1990s.

SPOOL BULLIES

House's small record labels, plucky as they were, couldn't hope to compete with the big boys, and duly the school bully of commercialization administered a wedgie to the UK house scene. Bastardized house songs, like M/A/R/R/S' 'Pump Up The Volume', infested the charts like scabies mites, while PLCs organized that oxymoron, 'commercial raves', in London's surrounding countryside. These introduced anthemic songs like 808 State's 'Pacific State' to the market consumers. While the experience of these open-air raves was authentic enough, the motivation behind them was anything but: they were moneymaking ventures pure and simple. So were a succession of cynical and substandard record releases that included Big Fun's appalling, but strangely also rather charming cover of the Jacksons' 'Blame it on the Boogie' – but hit new levels of effluvia with two records that should hang their grooves in shame even for existing. These are the most atrocious records ever to sully the shelves of Virgin Megastore. They are utter, utter shit. They are 'Swing the Mood' and 'That's What I Like', both by Jive Bunny. Never has myxomatosis seemed so appealing.

GO WEST

By the early 1990s, the UK rave scene was stagnating, so the resident US disc jockeys – along with some British colleagues who fancied making it big Stateside – traversed the big pond and took rave with them. One of these American DJs was the soon-to-be-infamous Frankie Bones. This is when the fun really started.

The first US raves took place in the Californian hippie havens of San Francisco and Los Angeles. If that's where they'd stopped, they'd not have caused a ripple in the dessert course. Californians put up with any old weirdness; that's their job.

SPIN AND BONES

It's when Frankie Bones took rave on tour that it became a US phenomenon. First he took rave to Brooklyn and held the Stormrave parties of 1992, where budding disc jockeys like Doc Martin, Kooki, Sven Vath and Josh Wink made their debuts. On to New York, where a crowd of 5000 kids gathered at a Queens loading dock for the biggest rave to date. It was at this seminal ecstasy-soaked event that the four keywords of both rave and ecstasy use were first uttered: 'Peace, Love, Unity, Respect' (PLUR). Disciples carried the gospel across the 50 states, and thousands of kids invited rave into their lives.

BRITFLOP

Back in the UK, and in the true spirit of the European Union, Italian bands were attempting to resurrect British house music. Mostly they failed, because their releases were just substandard covers of UK and US releases, but with the song 'Ride on Time' by Black Box – an excellent track whereby the vocals of Loleatta Holloway's 'Love Sensation' were applied to a keyboard background – the Italians really came up with the goods. The British public duly rewarded Black Box by keeping their song at Number One for a phenomenal five weeks.

The British record-buying public was not always so discerning: 'Ride On Time' had to usurp a four-week run of Jive Bunny to gain chart ascendancy. A year or so later the record-buying public effectively delayed the meeting of *The Simpsons* and UK sophisticates by introducing the yellow folk via the appalling sub-house track 'Do The Bartman', which occupied the top spot in early 1991.

IT ALL SOUNDS THE SAME

Something subcultures have in common is the axiom from outsiders and old folk that the music 'all sounds the same', a stance that only fortifies the culture to its adherents. To an outsider there is a far greater difference between Black Sabbath's 'War Pigs' and Metallica's 'For Whom The Bell Tolls' than there is between 'War Pigs' and Louis Armstrong's 'All the Time in the World'. However, for your common or garden headbanger the similarities between the decade-apart metal songs are equivalent to those between orange chalk and a markedly blue brand of cheese.

By the early '80s, up to 4,000 therapists in the US and Switzerland were using MDMA, known as 'penicillin for the soul'. A survey of therapists using it at the time, carried out in 1990, found that over three-quarters believed that the drug had 'great overall psychological value'.

Punk rock was the definitive 'it all sounds the same' music, but in retrospect even a Martian happening upon the genre must recognize a chasmic distance in style between The Clash's 'White Man In Hammersmith Palais' and The Stranglers' 'Nice And Sleazy'.

Basically, the 'it all sounds the same to me' aphorism is prejudiced bollocks – with one exception. Rave music does its level best to beat those bollocks. It doesn't take prejudgment or old-fashioned values to find rave tracks indistinguishable from one another. Even open-minded individuals – those who will try anything once, except fucking nuns and line dancing – can leave a rave with the impression of having listened to just the one song, nay the one beat, over its eight-hour duration. In a sense that's exactly what they have done – if the disc jockey's any good.

DJ HOOKERS

Disc jockeys have come a long way since they didn't jockey discs. The original Jamaican DJs had an assistant, the 'selector', to handle the trivial matter of choosing and playing records. While the selector spun his favourite ska and reggae tunes, the DJ would 'toast': add vocal effects to the pre-recorded track. Looking toward posterity, DJs soon started to make recordings of their toasts over their selectors' mix. This became known as dub, an abbreviation of 'double'.

CONTEMPORARY DJS

Disc jockeys have moved on, and moved their audiences, in leaps and bounds since those voiceover days. Since then they have divided into three types, which of course can overlap, with one DJ participating in different areas, as follows:

- **Radio DJ segues** between radio tracks and more importantly gives a personality and identity to the radio station. It is usually the marketing committee in overall charge rather than the DJ himself/herself who selects the tracks to play. The radio DJ is therefore more an artiste (performing artist) than artist (creative artist).
- **Travelling DJ** – The ultimate improvizer, travels around emceeing raves and choosing tracks, and therefore must make a good first impression every time.
- **Club DJ** - Employed by a rave venue to entertain its particular crowd, and is therefore well-known by his/her collective audience and knows the particular 'crowd pleasers' that get it bopping. The easiest method to allow self-marketing by the DJ and develop him/her a reputation.

JOIN THE CLUB

Although all three categories of DJ are relevant to the history of rave it is the third - the club DJ - that is the absolute essence of the rave culture itself. Rave DJs are the equivalent of the live band at a gig. At a rave, the DJs *are* the act. They don't just put on records and listen through headphones, they are musicians in their own right. The good rave DJ is an improvizer par excellence; every bit as adept at thinking on his (usually it's a he) musical feet as Dizzy Gillespie on his favourite trumpet. He will spin the records with all the agility of a Neapolitan pizza chef handling a sticky lump of dough. He will pick up the vibes of that night's particular crowd and mix the music to match its mood; he will cause the songs to segue into one another, adjusting the speeds and pitches to produce, in effect, a single and original multi-hour musical track.

The individual ravers in turn will also improvize, interpreting the music with their bodies. In this sense there is a dichotomy at the heart of the rave experience: for all the documented spirit of comradeship - PLUR - the essence of rave dancing is one of solitude, of losing oneself in the music.

To these people there is a seismic difference between tracks within a single genre, let alone those between different ones. Those coming to rave anew from, say, Blur and Oasis would have the proverbial feline's chance in the infernal regions of telling house apart from Detroit techno, let alone Tortoise apart from Jazzanova. For these people I now provide a potted history of electronic music.

ELECTRIC MUSIC UNTIL THE CURRENT TIME

Electronic music dates to the ondes martenot used by classical composers like Olivier Messiaen in the 1940s but was pretty much a curiosity until Robert Moog invented the analogue synthesizer in 1965. Synthesized music inhabited the pretentious soundscapes of avant-gardes like Karlheinz Stockhausen and Steve Reich, until the late-1960s when bands like King Crimson and Pink Floyd brought it to the attention of students and the art set.

They may have resembled chartered surveyors, but the Herrn that comprised Kraftwerk have the entire electronic sound in their favour, because they introduced electronic sounds into mainstream popular music with their albums *Autobahn* and *The Man Machine*, as well as individual tracks like 'Trans Europe Express'. Other European artists like Tangerine Dream and Jean-Michel Jarre leaped aboard this electric-powered bandwagon, and paved the way for late 1970s/1980s artists like Brian Eno, The Human League, Ultravox and Gary Numan to do their electronic thing.

PARTS OF RAVE

Electronic rave music comprises one or more of the following components (some of these definitions are decidedly different from the usual ones):

- **Drums** - Any sounds (other than the bass ones) that give rhythm to a song - in rave music that is just about all of them;
- **Samples** - Short extracts mixed into a different backing track, or recorded sounds fed into a synthesizer to be replayed at differing pitches. Sampled sounds are often harvested from perversely differing sources: for example, Beats International's 'Dub Be Good To Me' includes both the bassline of The Clash's 'Guns Of Brixton' and Charles Bronson's harmonica theme from Sergio Leone's Western *Once Upon A Time In The West;*
- **Computer-Generated Drums (CGD)** - Not to be confused with the generic 'drums' category described above, these are specific synthesized drum sounds from a computer or electronic drum machine;
- **Traditional Bass** - Synthesized electric or acoustic double-bass sounds, used in nearly all rave tracks;
- **303 bass** - Bass sounds that don't try to emulate non-electronic instruments - again, used in nearly all rave music;
- **Traditional Keyboards And Strings** - Synthesized piano, organ, guitar and violin sound used to give melody and substance to the music's drum and bass beat;
- **Synth Sounds** - specifically, those that resemble nothing else bar a synthesizer - the synthesizer saying, 'Screw this for a lark' to emulation, and producing its own sounds for its own sounds' sake;
- **Traditional Vocals** - Some girl or geezer singing into a microphone;
- **Computer Voices** - Robotic lyrics (ie when it sounds like *Doctor Who*'s Davros is spinning the discs).

RAVE CATEGORIES

Categorizing rave music is particularly futile and inaccurate, but here goes...

- **Acid House** - House with the addition of Roland 303 synthesizers that produces different pitches and layers.
- **Detroit Techno** - Influenced by European electrobeat: high bass levels, fast pace of 115-300 beats per minute (bpm). In two words, 'fast and pounding'. Too pounding to retain the soul of house, according to purists. It certainly severed the link between house and disco.

- **Hardcore Techno** – As Detroit techno, but even faster and even more pounding.
- **Gabba Techno** – Of Dutch provenance, this is the fastest and most pounding of the techno trinity. The very soul of 'fast and pounding', with speeds that can exceed 1,000bpm. The disturbing samples added to this subgenre – screams of terror reminiscent of snuff movies and suchlike – tend to detract from any feel-good factor.
- **Breakbeat** – Hip-hop samples and reggae tunes with fast beats and high-pitched samples.
- **Jungle** – Percussion, bongos, ragga vocals and samples.
- **Darkside** – Choral progressions that create a dark urban sound.
- **Trance** – Slow, melodic and hypnotic. Take out the pacifier/dummy and smooch your smelly friend. Halfway house between the hardcore of Moby and the ambience of Brian Eno. Each new day seems to see a lengthening on the list of 'silly subgenres with trance in the name': hard trance, acid trance, trancecore, Goa trance and psychedelic trance are some of the current ones.
- **Drum And Bass** – Hardcore techno spiced up with hip-hop, industrial sounds, ragga, jazz, funk and a speeded-up breakbeat sound. The return of 'fast and pounding': just when you thought is was safe to go back in the dance hall...

This list is both a generalization and a work in progress. Rave music is in a constant state of evolution, with new styles always being created.

RAVE IN THE US

Rave in the US is a part-time subculture for Generation X. Just as folk no longer see a job as a career and incline toward part-time or job-share work, the rave generation will tune in, turn on and drop out for the weekend, then turn up to work on Monday. (Then put in a poor working week until Wednesday due to the extended hangover that is peculiar to E; see Chapter 4.) Accordingly the US rave scene typically comprises white, middle-class youths in the 17- to 25-year-old age bracket, with an equal divide between boys and girls.

Of course a subculture is nothing without some anti-establishment sticking-up of the erect middle finger toward authority. In US rave, the behind-the-bike-sheds combined naughtiness of breaking into warehouses and consuming a Class A drug gives rave its *raison d'être*. Breaking into US warehouses is an out-and-out crime in the US, as opposed to its piddling UK trespassing equivalent that merely lands the perpetrators with the proverbial rapped knuckles. This has led to the US 'rave hop', whereby one rave can take place over several venues over a single night: 200 kids may set up speakers on a private beach, drop some Es, crank up the volume and bop till the cops come calling. They then move on to the next venue – a warehouse say – and so forth until daybreak puts an end to the hide-and-seek japery.

RAVE FASHIONS

The rave fashion is one of individuality, a fact that makes any attempt to describe it another 'big generalization'. Another 'here goes' is therefore in order.

The subtext of rave fashions is one of regression to childhood. It sticks a young child's chocolate-smeared middle finger of innocence up to authority, resenting that such innocence has been corrupted by self-centred adult concerns. Clothing and accessories are chosen to reinforce these kindergarten capers, though there is also a practical dimension to some of these clothes preferences. Typical boy's attire includes baggy pants and cartoon-character T-shirts. Girls favour tomboy cropped hair and baby-doll dresses. Accessories would be more suited to the floor of a crèche at late afternoon – ravers will happily wield cuddly toys, glowsticks and babies' pacifiers without the slightest concern that they personally might look ridiculous. The dummies also have another, rather unsavoury, practical use (see p119).

CLUBAL NEGATIVE

Not everyone is overwhelmed by the rave experience. This correspondent feels that the initial rave spark has well and truly been extinguished: 'I'm still down with the music, which i kind of accidentally discovered, but the scene is pretty much a joke. no it is a joke. i can imagine it was pretty dope when it was completely underground and peoples' motives were pure.

but the whole things a cliche now, a total parody of itself. the party is indeed over when kids on soap operas are going to "raves." and anything that needs an acronym to remind people how to act is bound to fail. it should be a given. sorry to rain on the parade, but bonnaroo [a Tennessee music festival held in June 2002] is right around the corner!'

RAVE IN THE UK

The rave culture in Blighty is both the same as and different from the US one. The fashions and 'reversion to childhood' theme is present in all its juvenile glory, and the social demographics are also similar. Research at Glasgow University suggests that 14.5 per cent of children from professional-class families had tried ecstasy and similar drugs at least once, as opposed to 7.5 per cent of children from skilled-working-class families.

Unfortunately, some inherent differences between the US and UK societies have trickled like diarrhoea down upon the UK rave scene, with the consequent stinking consequences.

BOOZE AND PILLS

The UK rave culture has diverted from open-spaced venues like out-of-town warehouses to city nightclubs of varying pokiness and ventilation. This has immense health consequences and contributes to the far greater incidence of ecstasy-related fatalities in the UK than the US. There is also a greater booze culture in the UK; a consequence of counterproductive licensing laws, whereby people have to drink several pints of beer between the hours of 11pm and 11:20pm before tanking up again in a nightclub. This also has immense health consequences because, even by drug-mixing standards, a cocktail of booze and ecstasy can have disastrous (if not fatal) results.

Drinks manufacturers thoughtfully opened the booze culture to young, even underage, ravers by introducing a type of drink called an 'alcopop' that tastes like a fizzy drink but carries the same alcoholic kick as a large Scotch whisky. Promotion campaigns that exactly mirrored the 'reversion to childhood' rave motif of the E culture were devised to sell the drinks to youngsters. Brands known as Hooch, Two Dogs and Jammin' appeared in off licences; advertisements featuring two border collies or a giant leering lemon were posted on hoardings. The latterday alcopop demographic has become synonymous with the rave culture. This, despite government efforts to enforce drinks companies to target a more mature market, has decidedly unhealthy ramifications.

GENERATION STOPGAP

It's not all bad, though. The UK rave culture has in effect joined two generations or rather both ends of the same one - the Generation X - in the PLUR ideals. An historical headstart over the US has resulted in people from the first wave of rave - when 'Ride on Time' and 'Dub Be Good to Me' were the dance tracks of choice - who are now in their 30s but still attend clubs to bop alongside the young'uns. A 36-year-old, London-based charity worker has this to say on the subject: 'I like to think I've covered most types of clubbing. I've gone to free festivals. In a squat party in Farringdon I came across the toilet to challenge [Irvine Welsh's book] *Trainspotting*'s "Worst Toilet in the World" - and when you've taken E sometimes you've just got to go! I've had the joy of feeling like one of the chosen people of God as the sun has come up on a Welsh valley having danced through the night (although seeing what your fellow dancers look like "when the lights go up" is always a frightening experience). I've danced with the beautiful people in the Ministry of Sound, somehow managing to smuggle myself past the fashion police on the door. Most of the time, however, I tend to go to smaller clubs that play hard house (music that is stripped down to very basic repetitive beats) like Mass or the 414 Club in Brixton. These tend to have small chill-out rooms where you can smoke dope and chat to people who are affable in the true rave scene stereotype. Although the clubs tend to be mainly male (hard house seems to be much more a "man thing"), and some look like they've just piled out of the pub the club still gives off a pleasant vibe so that you can chat to people. The majority are nearly all modern, urban hippies in one form or another (girls in short tie-died dresses and big boots, guys in t-shirts & combat pants). It is still refreshing how no-one really dresses up to go to these clubs (unlike some of the bigger London clubs). It is even more refreshing that despite being predominantly the home of people in the 20s, or even teens, that there are still enough veterans like ourselves around to not stand out (maybe it's the chill out area that attracts us in larger numbers). I hear that the big London super-clubs have become more the home ground of mid-30s coke-snorting executives (many still in their suits).'

THIS REALLY IS ECSTASY

Of course, the point of discussing the rave culture is that it is – or at least was until recently – effectively the same thing as the ecstasy culture. You cannot understand one without the other.

NEBULOUS NOMENCLATURE

In the one sense, ecstasy carries the least confusing nomenclature of all the street drugs. Unlike the multitude and ever-growing number of slang terms for, say, cannabis, generic ecstasy is only known by the names 'ecstasy', 'E,' 'adam' and MDMA. In another esoteric sense, it does no such thing. Any punter looking for technical information about the drug might have *these* beauties to contend with:

- MDMA;
- MDM;
- N-methyl-MDA;
- 3,4-methylenedioxymethamphetamine;
- N-methyl-3,4-methylenedioxyamphetamine;
- N-methyl-3,4-methylenedioxyphenylisopropylamine;
- N,alpha-dimethyl-3,4-methylenedioxyphenethylamine;
- N,alpha-dimethyl-1,3-benzodioxole-5-ethanamide;
- N,alpha-dimethyl-homopiperonylamine;
- N-methyl-1-(3,4-methylenedioxyphenyl)-2-propanamine;
- 2-methylamino-1-(3,4-methylenedioxyphenyl)-propanamine;
- N-methyl-beta-(3,4-methylenedioxyphenyl)-isopropylamine;
- N,alpha-dimethyl-beta-(3,4-methylenedioxyphenyl)-ethylamine;
- EA-1475;
- DEA Control #7287: MDMA HCl;

- DEA Control #7405: MDMA;
- DEA Control #7406: MDMA;
- Chem Abs: [66142-89-0] S-(+)-MDMA;
- Chem Abs: [69558-32-3] S-(+)-MDMA HCl;
- Chem Abs: [81262-70-6] R-(-)-MDMA;
- Chem Abs: [69558-31-2] R-(-)-MDMA HCl;
- Chem Abs: [69610-10-2] MDMA;
- Chem Abs: [64057-70-1] MDMA HCl.

ROLL ON

There is no longer such thing as an ecstasy trip. There used to be, when the drug was in its early dance days and ravers were too caught up in their own euphoria to compare notes, but no longer. The experience is still there, of course – MDMA hasn't suddenly lost all its narcotic qualities. It's just that seasoned ravers reckoned that the name didn't fit the experience and changed it to 'roll'. A correspondent – the superbly named Saint Jude, Patron of Lost Causes – writes: 'God only knows where it started, but the terms really fits...rolling, as in moving along with little effort on sheer momentum. Once the drug's effects start it usually just...well, rolls right along on it's own...you don't feel like you're really making an investment of effort in whatever you're doing.'

ROLLING IN THE AISLES

The rave culture is inexorably linked with ecstasy. The two are symbiotic; they effectively inhabit the same cultural gaff. There are exceptions, but these are of the type that apparently proves a rule. Most notable are the 'raves in the nave' organized by trendy vicars. Here young Christian folk (by invitation) break into cathedrals and hold a sweaty bop. They class it as an act of worship: it is their equivalent of sleeping during the sermon and mouthing the hymns because you can't reach the pitch of the women around you. A Methodist minister, the Reverend Jeff Reynolds, raves over the holy antics to be had in the aisles: 'After many years of being involved with various events as an organizer and performer it was good to visit Ely Cathedral as a "punter". It was my first visit to "Rave in the Nave" and it was a very pleasurable experience. From wondering whether I would squeeze my six-foot-three [1.9m], 15 stone [95kg] frame into a Velcro suit, to not being particularly turned on by my blackcurrant cordial and orange juice type cocktail (enough to turn anyone to drink!), to casting a musician's eye over the band, to being particularly moved by the different types of worship in the Lady Chapel, I found the event stimulating and refreshing. It was great to stand in that beautiful building and realise that for centuries worship has evolved and provoked a response from worshippers. This event was no different and thank God that we can worship in a style that is relevant to our modern culture. Yes, I'll definitely be back, all I need is a bigger Velcro suit, a stamp that actually works on my hand and more imagination in the cocktail line!'

Not everyone's cup of blackcurrant-cordial-and-orange-juice-type cocktail, for sure.

JUVENIL-E DELINQUENCY

So, is ecstasy a delinquent's drug? Does it involve internecine ghetto gang warfare, muggings, pimping, prostitution, selling your grandparents to feed the habit? Nope, ecstasy will have none of that. Not at the user level. Not until recently (see pp58–9).

Is ecstasy a hippie drug? Does it favour abandonment of material wealth, 'tuning in, turning on and dropping out' and open-air festivals in the pissing-down rain? Yes, but only half-heartedly. Like rave, ecstasy is a part time pursuit. A Mancunian correspondent and Hacienda veteran writes the following: 'So is E addictive? Well in my experience raving certainly is. My friends and I early on vowed to sensibly manage our raving. The anticipation and high was so great, and the washed-out feeling from dancing all night potentially so low that it required limits on how frequently we would rave. Most of this was down to the fact that we mostly had jobs requiring responsibility during work hours (our group includes everything from a company director to a barrister). This certainly meant that money wasn't a problem (we'd hardly be stealing off old ladies to fund our rave habit), but coping with the come-down on Monday was. For the same reason we never took too many Es in one night (there is always a temptation in a long night to take another as the first is wearing off, and then inevitably another, or just to increase the dose). I remember being with someone at an outdoor rave whose middle-distance stare and brain-dead responses in the morning showed the dangers of taking too many.'

Ecstasy is not heroin: its users do not base their entire lives around the drug, living in derelict council estates, claiming social security and stealing stereo systems. No, they take the drug at weekends, then turn up to work on Monday. This involves a sleep-deprivation hangover of phenomenal proportions.

GO TO WORK ON AN E

Alternatively, some ecstasy users attempt to prolong the euphoria; to continue the rave into Monday. Unfortunately, there's a minor irritant called work that gets in the way. An 18-year-old shop worker sent me this account of E-induced crust-earning: 'This was yesterday; I can't believe we got away with it, me and a girl at work on half an ecstasy each! I don't think I'd get away with it again though. NEVER again. The girl who I'll call "I" suggested doing a pill at work, I said half each, we agreed. It was one of those "I'll do it if you will" type things. I went for my break at around 10:40am and ate as much as I possibly could. Went to the kitchen to get a knife, took that to the toilet to cut the pill. Did that, swallowed half, and put the other half back in the bag, which went in my pocket. Back to work, spoke to "I" handed her the contents of my pocket. I don't think she was expecting me to do it, but she followed my lead and went for a break. As "I" left, the duty manager arrived and was on the till with me. How ironic! There I was, taking E at work for the first time, and the most anti-drugs person I know was standing six inches [15cm] away serving customers with me! I felt okay so far, I could feel the effects of it, but because I was concentrating it wasn't overpowering. I didn't get stressed at all. The great thing about my job is

1985, the US Drug Enforcement Administration placed MDMA in the most restrictive category of controlled substances. This therapeutic tool, had 'leaked out into the general community to become ecstasy, the party drug'.

the ability to play what I like. I'm not really bothered if the customer's don't like it! "I" was shelf filling, obviously staying away from the tills. Every time I looked at her, she would smile, giggle a bit and I would smile back, it was like that all afternoon. The duty manager had no idea whatsoever. I was nice and friendly to all the customers all day, and got no complaints about my attitude or music selection. And the best thing about it? Well, at 5:30pm just as we were leaving the new manager came over and praised us for our hard work, the first time I have been thanked for doing a good job in three and a half years!'

And they say drugs are bad... I'll leave you to make your own conclusion.

SYNONYMITY

With exceptions like 'rave in the nave', rave is ecstasy and vice versa (though that 'is' is worryingly becoming a 'was' in this third millennium). Like LSD to the hippies and speed to the punks, ecstasy is a drug whose effects exactly induce the emotions carried by the subculture's ideals. Whether ecstasy or rave came first is to invite recursive comparisons between chickens and eggs. However, it is clear that ecstasy and PLUR go together like the (brand of E tablet) 'strawberries and cream'. McCready writes of the first encounters of Hacienda patrons to the new drug:

> *According to Shaun and Bez [respectively Shaun Ryder, the singer with, and 'Bez', the dancer with, seminal Manchester indy band Happy Mondays], interviewed some time after the event and not usually known for being good with dates, some of their mates had been away on holiday in Valencia and Ibiza and had brought back some ecstasy tablets. People tried them out and they seemed to fit the music perfectly. Many lost their inhibitions overnight – feeling comfortable enough to get on stages and podiums and wave their arms about in a state of, well, ecstasy – hearing things in the music that they couldn't hear before. A new low-rent crowd started mixing with the converted hairdressers and Factory obsessives of old. It was, at times, a volatile mix. But the drugs turned an often socially confused crowd into one sweaty nation, under the influence of a*

groove twisted out of a small silver box (the Roland 303) invented by Japanese technicians to provide a kind of karaoke backing for social-club country-and-western singers.

NEW DRUG ON THE BLOCK

LSD, the powering drug of rave's yellow-smiley-faced predecessor acid house, was hardly conducive to a evening's social merriment, inducing as it does 12 hours of hallucinations, distorted colours and occasional freakouts and attempts to fly out of upstairs windows.

Just as well ecstasy was diverted from its original purpose. Ecstasy, real name '3, 4 Methylenedioxymethamphetamine' (MDMA), was developed as a psychotherapeutic drug to promote empathy and reduce hostility between estranged spouses. It was a marriage-guidance drug and still is in Switzerland (see Chapter 3 on the history of MDMA).

SERENDIPITY

Ecstasy's discovery by pioneering boppers was accidental, but once young folk used to freaking on acid discovered its euphoric effect there was no stopping E as a dance drug. MDMA is the ideal inspiration for the rave culture because on the one sweaty hand it encourages communal empathy with one's fellow humans and, on the other sweaty paw, induces a blissful isolated communion between the dancer and the techno beat.

EAT SHIT

There's one problem, though. The shit that it's mixed with does no such thing. Happily that last sentence is not literal...yet. E tablets do not so far constitute combined MDMA and dehydrated cat-litter foragings, but the substances they do contain don't fall far short in nastiness. Delightful substances found co-inhabiting an ecstasy tablet alongside the MDMA include fish-tank cleaners and dog-worming tablets – as well as other drugs like LSD, caffeine and antihistamine and even the poison strychnine. There is an increasing incidence of adulterated E tablets appearing on the streets because of greater competition between drug traffickers (see Chapter 2). Shit, after all, is the drug dealer's bread and butter.

A US correspondent has this to say (you might get bogged down with drug abbreviations, but you can't fail to get his gist): 'The biggest problem is that street E may not be pure MDMA. If you speed too much, suspect meth or meth plus MDMA. If you dissociate, suspect PCP or K. You should get some empathic feelings and back rubs should be heaven. Even empathic feelings don't mean E, could be MDA or MDEA. They've found some pills that were a mix of 6 things, MDMA, meth, pcp, k and I can't remember what else. Sometimes you get crap like bzp, tfmpp, or dxm which can be bought legally for a hell of lot less than 30 bucks [£20] a pill. Sometimes you get stuff with trace amounts or with nothing. Buy from a reputable dealer. Watch out for deadly PMA [para-methoxyamphetamine - a toxic amphetamine].'

It is therefore paramount for kids investing their pocket money in a couple of yellow pills to scan them for shit before eating them. Paramount, maybe, but also well-nigh impossible without expert advice. (See Chapter 5 about proposed government moves to provide this.)

BRAND LOYALT-E

E tablets are like washing powder, and not only because they might contain washing soda alongside the MDMA. Ecstasy inspires brand loyalty; and accordingly new brands of essentially the same stuff are increasingly cluttering up the black marketplace, with low-level dealers attempting to push the individual benefits of their own product.

Ecstasy comes in small tablets the size of a headache tablet, or else in capsule form, and consists of MDMA combined with other substances to make up the weight. (There is also some inherent adulteration in ecstasy pills because of the binding agents used to press the pills.) Sometimes, the MDMA part of the tablet is in fact an analogue substance like the parent drug MDA that induces a more intense experience.

Though all basically the same thing, the tablets come in a massive variety of colours, with a massive variety of motifs embossed on them and a massive range of brand names to reflect the 'reversion to childhood/innocence reborn' ethos. There is consequently a three-times-massive marketplace of competitive E brands.

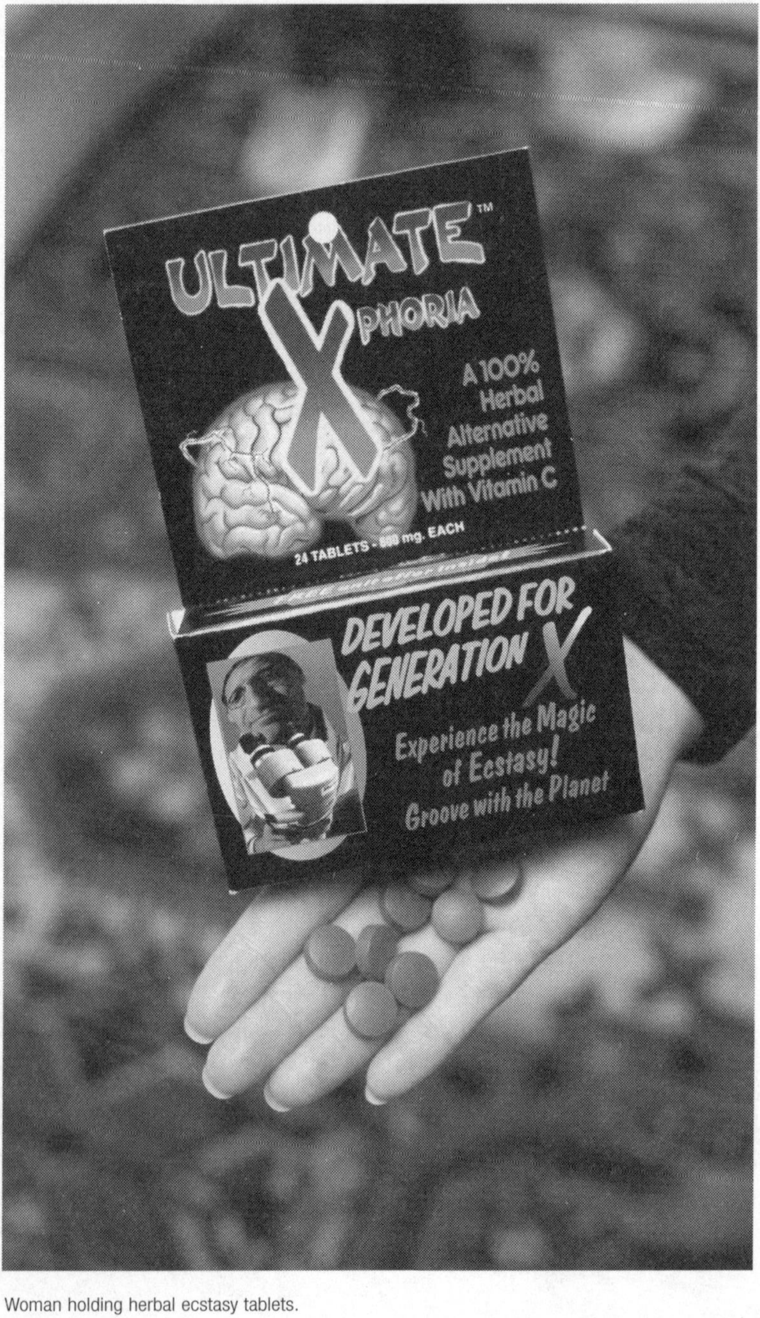

Woman holding herbal ecstasy tablets.

Customs officer Carsten Kallmann shows off bags filled with ecstasy pills in Düsseldorf, after the 199,000 pills with a black-market value of some five million DM were seized from a 49-year-old businessman in January 1999.

A BRIEF GUIDE TO E

Here's a look at some current E brands, including their names, their design and the particular childhood memories they attempt to tap into. Given the ever-increasing enormity of brands on offer, this is by necessity just the thin end of the iceberg or, to put it another way, the tip of the wedge. Ecstasy brands fall into different categories that purport to fulfil different purposes.

PURITY OF DRUG

These supposedly let on what's inside the pill to reassure nervous consumers that they're getting what they're paying for. Don't believe a word of it. Take a look at the following examples.

- **Triple X** - MDMA and its two analogues, MDA and MDEA.
- **Madman** - Pure MDMA (assonant with 'adam', an older name for MDMA).
- **Madwoman** - Pure MDEA.
- **Adam And Eve** - MDMA and MDEA.
- **Eva** - Tablets with letters 'E' embossed on one side and 'A' on the other; contains amphetamine plus MDMA.
- **K Capsules** - Contain MDMA plus ketamine.
- **China White** - May contain '3-methylfentanyl' a very potent heroin substitute known under the same street name as the ecstasy pill.
- **Coke Biscuit** - Implication that pill contains cocaine - unlikely, because there couldn't be enough included to vivify a gnat.

STRENGTH OF DRUG

Sod the purity - how wasted will it get you?

- **E 130** - Capsule with 'E 130' printed on the side; 10mg stronger than typical MDMA dose of 120mg.
- **Pink 125** - Pink tablet; 5mg stronger than typical dose of 120mg.
- **Phase 4** - MDMA plus sufficient amphetamine to keep you manic for four hours.
- **Phase 8** - As 'phase 4' but twice as speedy.

SHAPE

Because, after all, appearance matters.

- **Snowballs** - Rough-edged, almost spherical pill; don't eat the yellow ones.
- **Disco Burgers** - Like most tablets, shaped like a hamburger - but coloured brown to add the Big Mac look.
- **Coke Burger** - As above, but imagine there's an oversized beaker containing mostly ice with it (rumours, as with 'coke biscuit' above, that the pills contain cocaine are unlikely to be true).
- **New Yorker** - Recalls yet another brand of hamburger - one that hasn't yet crossed the big pond eastwards.
- **Biscuits** - Big, flat and granular. None to date include a cream filling.

COLOUR CONNOTATION

Since the Coca-Cola Company supposedly redesigned Santa Claus to wear its own trademark red and white brand colours, canny promoters have used connotation to market their products. Ecstasy manufacturers are no exception.

- **M25** - Pink with a blue stripe across the middle vice versa. (If this is how ecstasy users view motorways, then maybe there is a further case for long-term brain damage than is described in Chapter 4.)
- **Manchester United** - Red and black to (wrongly) match the colours of the soccer team supported by everyone worldwide except the people of Manchester (who support City).
- **Dennis The Menace** - Red and black to match the colours of the *Beano* comic-strip rapscallion; possibly the same pill as Manchester United, marketed toward the die-hard inhabitants of the 'regression to childhood' set.

SECONDS OF PUDDING/FIRST IN LINE AT THE TUCK SHOP

The ultimate reversion to childhood motif - recalls those days asking for more crumble in the canteen, or buying sherbet in the tuck shop.

- **Rhubarb And Custard** – Red and yellow pills that recall the most repulsive dessert course ever devised by man (one source suggests that the 'barb' part of the name indicates that the pill contains barbiturate).
- **Love Hearts** – Variably coloured pills with a heart embossed in the centre; memories of passing a sherbety sweet to the girl in ponytails and mouth braces come flooding back (these allegedly contain the tranquillizer methaqualone alongside the MDMA).
- **Banana Splits** – Yellow and white pills to remind you of the syrupy reward for eating all your greens at restaurants; older ravers may also recall the goofy animal characters Fleegle, Snorky, Bingo and Drooper, or at least The Dickies' cover of their theme song.
- **Strawberries And Cream** – Pink and white pills that relive lazy summer afternoons watching Becker versus Lendl in the Wimbledon men's tennis finals.
- **Strawberries** – Straight pink versions of the above pills for lactose-intolerants.
- **Parma Violets** – Purple tablets that evoke small chalky sweets with indeterminate flavour that were occasionally bought out of curiosity and vomited out of necessity.

CARTOON CHARACTERS

This is the other ultimate reversion-to-childhood motif, harking back to the days when Saturday mornings were spent not in bed but downstairs watching television.

- **Super Mario** – Plumb the depths of euphoria.
- **Superman** – Is it a bird? Is it a plane? No, it's an angular letter S embossed on a pill.
- **Pink Panther** – Did you ever see a tablet ever so pink?
- **Batman** – *Powww! Thuddd! Thwaappp!*
- **Bart Simpson** – Eat my shorts.
- **Mickey Mouse** – Join the club.
- **Donald Duck** – Send you quackers.

EMBOSSED

More reputable than burgers, biscuits or sweets. Embossed shapes, designs or logos afford ecstasy tablets a supposed quality trademark, like the 'By royal appointment' stamps on jars of marmalade. They are also harder to fake.

- **P And T** – Pete Tongs (after a UK disc jockey), Partick Thistle (Scottish football team), 'party timers' or 'peeping toms'.
- **Shamrocks** – So Irish you can taste the poteen.
- **Love Doves** – the definitive PLUR drug; comes in several varieties to reflect the bird's comportment, including 'both wings up', 'both wings down', 'one wing up and one wing down', 'double doves' (which are embossed both sides) and the transmogrifying 'white robin'.
- **Euro** – € sign embossed on the pill.
- **Smiley** – White with acid house face.
- **VW** – Yellow or grey with Volkswagen logo.

DOSE OF CRAP

The typical E dose to sustain a night's bopping is a single tablet containing 75–150mg of what may or not be MDMA. This should take around 40 minutes before initiating a euphoric rush that resides to an empathic happiness. Ecstasy is not really a hallucinogen, though some of the aforementioned shit it's mixed with might be.

For some users the oral ingestion of ecstasy has become decidedly passé. They yearn to offer their other orifices a bit of the action. To them the mouth is *so* 1997.

Snorting, smoking and injecting are the most popular alternatives. All are of varying dangerousness and predictability; and the first one, which involves crushing up E tablets with a razor blade, leaves users blowing a cocktail of snot and shards into their handkerchief for days.

The most extreme and apparently quite sensational non-oral method of ecstasy ingestion is that of 'plugging': to follow the example of the suppository and take the instruction 'Stick it up your arse' a tad too literally. This is a logistical nightmare (though presumably the baggy pants help); but those bold adventurers in the realm of ecstatic anal application report a 30 per cent slower release time and an accordant extension of the initial euphoric rush.

Regular ecstasy users are 25 per cent more likely to suffer a mental health disorder than the rest of the population, according to what is believed to be the most extensive survey of clubbers published yesterday. One in four had a potentially serious psychiatric disorder, compared to the national average of less than one in five, the survey of 1,000 clubbers, in the dance culture magazine *Mixmag*, revealed.

A US contact once inquired about one of the most profound, nay metaphysical, concerns surrounding anal ecstasy insertion: how to keep the tablet inserted up your back passage without it falling out again. He writes: 'It would have to be a pretty damn good time to convince me to stick a pill up my ass. (Plus if it falls back out you can't exactly change your mind and decide to eat it.) If it is that great, what's the procedure anyway, do you just sort of stick it up there and try not to take a shit for a couple hours?'

HEALTHY RAVING

The health implications of ecstasy use are explained in detail in Chapter 4. At this juncture it is only necessary to point out that the likelihood of the drug being what you think it is is not high – unless you have a trusted and regular dealer.

THE NEW WAVE OF RAVE AND ECSTASY

The last few years have seen some unprecedented violence at street level, including seizure of weapons, shootouts with police in NYC and Detroit, and even internecine murder between dealers (see pp73–4).

Rave is still inexorably an ecstasy culture, but the reverse is no longer the case. Ecstasy is increasingly available in schools and private homes; it is no longer just a club drug. This has led to a wider user base and age range. People over 40 now regularly drop E, especially former cocaine users who reckon that ecstasy carries similar euphoric qualities, lasts longer and is safer. This has raised the interest of crack and heroin dealers – an altogether more insalubrious lot than the chumps who formerly palmed some E for their mates – and is currently dragging the E trade into the same gangland shit as its opium-based siblings.

To appreciate the process that has brought about this situation, we need to look at the world of ecstasy.

02 WORLD

TWIN DILEMMA

With a terrible beauty, the twin towers of New York's World Trade Center collapsed like dominoes, interring 10,000 innocent souls in a mass grave. Some took their death in their own hands and jumped from high windows to save being crushed under the rubble. Firefighters earned a crust that never came as they perished alongside their white-collar compatriots.

Soon, the tributes arrived: enemies from both sides of the Middle East conflict united to express their disgust; Royal Guardsmen played the 'Star Spangled Banner' while American tourists wept behind the railings; nations grieved; and planes were grounded. The trafficking of ecstasy into the US stopped completely.

Three weeks later, it started up again. These ravers can't wait for ever, you know.

GROUND FORCE

The events of 11 September 2001 were a real downer for the ecstasy smugglers. The grounding of passenger planes effectively nullified their usual mode of operation, leaving a lot of very unhappy punters worldwide. Even when planes were allowed to resume flight, the smugglers were reluctant to go back to work.

COMMERCIAL CONCERNS

Ecstasy is usually smuggled via commercial flights. The smugglers' problem in the weeks after the New York attacks was the paucity of commercial flyers. People were still shell-shocked from the television images and also fearful to fly for threat of further terrorist attacks. Vacationers suddenly lost their appetite for sun and fun, while commuters chose to travel overland rather than risk the air. Planes became decidedly empty, security became decidedly vigilant...and drugs couriers became decidedly conspicuous.

One of the major destinations for ecstasy smugglers is Newark Airport in New Jersey, mainly on account of its nine daily flights from The Netherlands (still the source of most MDMA manufacture). Thomas Manifase, a special agent in charge of its Customs Investigation Office, writes of this period: 'I think the smugglers sensed the intense inspections and shut down their operations.'

This enforced cessation of ecstasy smuggling led to the mother of all back orders in the US and UK. It dealt mid-level-dealers a loss of income that would leave foot-and-mouth-disease-stricken farmers looking like Bill Gates in comparison. It also deprived the rave generation of the fuel to power its bopping and hugging.

When operations started up again, on around 20 October 2001, it was as if a little Dutch boy had said to himself, 'Sod this for a lark,' and pulled his hand out of the dyke: unstoppable quantities of E flooded into airports worldwide. Manifase writes: 'Over half a million tablets were seized in seven-eight weeks... That's huge.' It's especially huge when added to the increase that's boarding the planes anyway. After all, a low-cost, high-profit industry like ecstasy trafficking was bound to take off in a big way.

MALIGNANT GROWTH

The word 'exponential' could have been devised to describe recent years' growth in ecstasy trafficking.

- In 1999, 3.5 million E tablets were seized; in 2000, the number was 9.3 million.
- In the US fiscal year (beginning 1 October and) ending 30 September 2001, 851,000 E tablets were seized at Newark Airport – twice as many as during the previous year.
- During fiscal year 2001 until December 2001, the seizures of MDMA at Newark Airport were already 65 per cent of the entire previous year.

- During the eight months prior to December 2001, seizures of ecstasy numbered over 542,000 tablets smuggled from Europe – a record number and a great concern to law enforcers.

NEW DRUGS IN OLD NEW ORLEANS

On 30 May 2000, George Cazenavette III, special agent in charge of the New Orleans Field Division of the US Drugs Enforcement Agency (DEA), released this statement to address his perception of increased ecstasy use in New Orleans:

> *In an effort to diminish the flow of drugs into this area, the New Orleans Field Division has dedicated six enforcement groups that actively investigate drug trafficking organizations responsible for the transportation and distribution of drugs throughout the metropolitan area.*

This was not an unqualified success. There was a subsequent arrest of ecstasy traffickers caught transporting MDMA from Houston, Texas to be distributed in New Orleans, Miami and New York. The group had passed on thousands of ecstasy tablets to local high-school and college students mostly at New Orleans raves. One defendant admitted to selling over 250,000 tablets during around 20 trips to New Orleans, each pill going for $10–15 (£7–10). Other defendants told of their smuggling techniques – they had hidden the pills on their person and carried them into cities on commercial airlines, then stashed them in secret storage vaults before separate runners carried them on to raves.

LAPD ACCRUES

On 26 July 2000, US federal agents intercepted 2.1 million ecstasy tablets, comprising nearly 500kg (1,100lb) of MDMA, valued at $40 million (£28 million), at Los Angeles International Airport. This was the biggest ecstasy bust to date. The drugs were found in 15 boxes on a flight from Paris, and comprised more than a quarter of the eight million ecstasy tablets seized in the US so far that year. By comparison, only 400 tablets of

MDMA were seized in the United States during the whole of 1997. 'That's 2.1 million tablets of ecstasy that won't go to our kids this year,' were the words of Stephen Wiley, the FBI special agent in charge of the strategy. The group responsible had been linked to other large global seizures, which included 300kg (700lb) of MDMA seized by US Customs in December 1999.

MEN IN WHITE

To understand why this growth is happening, we must first trace the ecstasy back to its source - a couple of geeks in a hidden laboratory.

In the flatlands of Holland and Belgium, an array of clandestine laboratories are to be found, producing MDMA on demand for an insatiable market. This may conjure images of white-coated henchmen working for Ernst Stavro Blofeld in hollowed-out volcanoes, but in reality a typical lab is likely to comprise a sordid bedsit with an electric stove, a kettle, an ashtray...and a high-speed commercial pill press. Alternatively, it could be a converted caravan - a mobile laboratory to allow MDMA makers a nifty escape from Inspector Knacker of Europol.

The natural advantages of setting up in Holland and Belgium include the following:

- Holland is a centre of the international chemical industry, so both personnel and certain precursor chemicals (a chemical that gives rise to another more important one) are readily available;
- Both countries have a state-of-the-art transport infrastructure and some of the world's busiest ocean ports.

Ecstasy users can at least take one crumb of narcotic comfort: the source MDMA inside their tablet was certainly synthesized by qualified chemists. Ecstasy traffickers demand the best from their manufacturers. Whether they deliver the best to their customers is another point entirely. MDMA manufacturers comprise graduate chemists, or at least experienced commercial lab technicians, who have, for their own nefarious reasons, allied with the dark side.

This is not to say that occasional DIY fanatics, who fancy a challenge beyond making rhubarb wine or ginger snaps, won't attempt to knock up a batch of MDMA in their kitchen. It's just that one of a) the kitchen, b) the DIY fanatic or c) both will be past history long before their version of MDMA can hit the streets. Recipes for MDMA are available on the Internet for those who really want them, including this one, seemingly written by someone on every drug known to mankind and a few known only to himself.

> Take the petals off the MDMA flower. Grind them up and boil in dilute H_2O. Let sit overnight and beautiful MDMA crystals will form.

THRALL WORLD

There are obviously logistical problems facing those who take the small-industry approach to MDMA manufacture. The majority of MDMA is therefore still made overseas in Holland and Belgium. Until recent years that last sentence could have read 'the vast majority...' Now it's just 'the majority...' Between the mid-1990s and 1999 these two countries accounted for 80 per cent of MDMA consumed worldwide, with little threat to their dominance despite the concerted efforts of law enforcers. Now other countries and continents are trying to muscle in.

Ecstasy works by stimulating serotonin production in the brain but in so doing damages the ability of the brain to produce serotonin in the future. People with low serotonin levels are likely to be depressed and commit suicide.

The greatest worry for US law enforcers is the opportunity for Mexican and Colombian traffickers to try and get in on the act. These countries have the same advantages that Belgium and the Netherlands have: availability of personnel and drugs; and (in this instance, overland) smuggling routes into the United States. Mexican Drug Trafficking Organizations (DTOs) even have an exemplar on which to base MDMA trafficking; the *hombres* have been shifting amphetamines into the States for years. Some Colombian and Mexican DTOs are certainly increasing their MDMA operations. For example, in 2000 a shipment of 60,000 ecstasy tablets was seized en route to the US.

Traffickers based in former Dutch colonies - the Dominican Republic, Netherland Antilles and Surinam - are also operating. They clearly have a respect for the traditions of their ancestors, these dudes.

CHEMISTRY DELICATESSEN

Chemists process MDMA using the constituent chemicals of safrole, piperonal and the snappily named '3,4 methylenedioxepenyl-2-propanone', which are illegally diverted from source countries including Germany, Poland, China and India. They synthesize MDMA in the form of a white powder, which is mixed with a binder like methyl cellulose (therefore E tablets are technically never pure MDMA), pressed into pills and packaged. Associate traffickers then sell them to mid-level wholesale distributors in quantities of at least 1,000, after which they are transported to distribution centres such as Houston, Jacksonville, Phoenix, Pittsburgh, Washington, DC and London.

DISTRIBUTION ROUTES

Although most distribution is to the US and UK, figures from the Vienna-based International Narcotics Control Board (INCB), which sent missions worldwide in 2001, found MDMA consumption and seizures increasing in continental Europe, east and Southeast Asia, Australia and New Zealand. The last two countries, in particular, suffered a steady increase in MDMA seizures due to a rising demand for the drug.

US law enforcers have tried to stop home-grown MDMA production at its source. A Department of State fact sheet included the following:

> *In addition to strict domestic controls on the chemicals required to manufacture ecstasy, the United States is working with the international community to deny traffickers access to the chemicals necessary for producing ecstasy. The 20-29 March 2001 meeting of the 53-member UN Commission on Narcotic Drugs adopted a resolution jointly sponsored by the United States and the 15 Member States of the European Union, outlining a number of measures governments should take jointly and individually to*

> *identify and control ecstasy and other synthetic drug chemicals. These measures include early warning systems to identify substitute chemicals being used in place of controlled chemicals, collaboration among laboratories to provide a better understanding of illicit manufacturing trends, and enhanced co-operation with the chemical industry.*

There is little indication that domestic MDMA production will expand much beyond the small number of low-production laboratories discovered each year in the United States. The requisite chemistry background and the difficulty in acquiring precursor and essential chemicals, combined with the current overflow of pills from Europe, make domestic production risky, less profitable and difficult for most people to accomplish. The overwhelming advantages enjoyed by production groups in the Netherlands and Belgium suggest that, in the near future, the vast majority of MDMA production will continue to be centred in the Benelux region – regardless of the level of demand in the United States or the accessibility to MDMA recipes on the Internet.

SMUGGLING METHODS

Drugs are of no use whatsoever sitting on their chemical arses in the source country. They need to be transported to other countries, where the authorities decidedly will not welcome their approach with open arms. It isn't just smuggling that's required, but the far more challenging task of 'smuggling without getting caught'.

These are the five methods of MDMA smuggling, in order of popularity.

COURIER

The nice thing about courier smuggling is that it caters for all abilities. People from all walks of life, from the timid chartered surveyor to the all-out mobster, can try their hand at it. All that is required is the will to succeed and some hot property to smuggle through. On the one warm hand we find (though hopefully customs don't) the occasional tippler taking a couple too many bottles of Languedoc plonk through the green channel, while on the other flame-spewing hand we find the heroin smuggler stitching several dozen bags of horse into the lining of his Armani jacket. Somewhere between these variably combusting versions of Mrs Palm and her five daughters – around abdomen level, say – we find the unwashed student boarding the ferry from Urnuiden to North Shields with a quarter ounce (7g) of cannabis stashed in his underpants.

Until recently the smuggling of ecstasy usually conformed to that last example, consisting as it did of entrepreneurial independent individuals smuggling through small amounts of E. However, the trend over the last couple of years has ominously tended toward methods akin to the heroin smuggler. In other words, the big boys have taken over.

Here, in descending order of seriousness, are some of the methods used to sneak MDMA past those pesky customs officials:

- Concealed in a false-bottomed suitcase;
- Fitted into the hollow heel of shoe;
- Hidden in hollowed-out furniture;
- Put in a baby carrier, and a baby put on top of it;
- Stitched into clothing;
- Taped to the torso or legs;
- Swallowed in a condom and then excreted in the host country.

This last one may bear consideration as a deterrent to any youngsters considering the E culture. The notion that their dove-embossed white pill may earlier have been foraged from someone's shit may give them cause for thought before swallowing it.

Once the pills are sneaked through customs and tipped out, unstitched or excreted, they are transported to distribution centres such as Houston, Jacksonville, Phoenix, Pittsburgh and Washington, DC.

Sadly for the drugs couriers trying to do an honest day's work, customs officials are suspicious fellows. Some of them even share a brain cell and have latched onto the fact that passengers on Dutch commercial flights may be carrying more than just miniature novelty windmills and hardcore porn. They have therefore targeted such flights for ecstasy surveillance.

To evade these quick-smart officials on the lookout for flying Dutchmen, trafficking organisations can divert couriers to one of three transit countries en route: Mexico, Canada and the Dominican Republic. Other roundabout routes include countries close to The Netherlands like Germany, Switzerland and France. The drugs are then transported to a hub city by plane. Hub cities include Atlanta, Los Angeles, Miami, New York and Newark.

The new and rising bands of Israeli and Russian DTOs have become particularly dab hands at smuggling MDMA via couriers. This is worrying to US drug enforcers, who are finding drugs from these sources increasingly harder to detect. There are a handful of cited reasons:

- These Israeli and Russian DTOs' operatives are borderline fanatics, and are unusually willing to follow their leaders' orders to the letter. They are therefore less likely to reveal sources if interrogated.
- The operatives are better trained and more proficient at smuggling than their European counterparts. Their smuggling profile is therefore greatly reduced.
- Recruitment of female couriers in preference to male ones deflects the attentions of the seemingly male chauvinist customs officials.
- Drug detection dogs frequently are not trained to sniff out the new-fangled MDMA. Israeli and Russian traffickers are well aware of this.

EXPRESS MAIL

There is one small problem with courier smuggling: people get caught doing it. This can have ramifications for the source manufacturers of the drug: law enforcers like nothing better than to take details of sources in return for putting in a favourable word with the trial judge.

A preferable method is to smuggle the contraband via much less suspicious sources, using people who don't know they're carrying it – postal delivery workers, for example. Send a stash of E via express mail and guarantee yourself overnight delivery courtesy of the Fed Ex company, and not to a stash site but directly to the mid- or low-level dealer. Again, it is Israeli and Russian groups that form the vanguard of this particular smuggling method and show those European slackers exactly how it should be done.

The apparently foolproof way of evading X-ray detection is to hide loose ecstasy tablets in amongst the pieces of a jigsaw puzzle. If those awkward bastards at customs do notice the strange proliferation of small circular jigsaw pieces on the scan (or else just like doing jigsaws) and therefore open the parcels to discover the rainbow assortment within, the traffickers should still remain anonymous (assuming they aren't stupid enough to use the dealer's real name or send it to his home address instead of a rented mailbox).

Traffickers can track the shipment through each stage of the shipping process by making use of the various express mail services' Internet facilities. If they notice that the package is being unusually delayed at any stage of the process, they'll assume it's been opened and give it up as a lost cause.

This extract from a report written by Lorraine Brown, the special agent in charge of the Office of Investigations US Customs Service, conveys the increasing frequency of MDMA being delivered by mail in recent years:

> *On 19 December 1999, inspectors at the Federal Express facility in Memphis, TN intercepted approximately 100lb [45kg] of MDMA destined for the Riverside, CA area. The RAIC/Riverside office, in conjunction with the Inland Regional Narcotics Enforcement Team, conducted a controlled delivery of the seized MDMA, resulting in the identification of an MDMA smuggling and distribution organization spanning two continents and five countries. The ensuing investigation led to execution of more than 12 search warrants, resulting in 13 arrests, the seizure of approximately 1.5 million tablets, $4,662,292 [£3,216,981] in US currency and $808,472 [£557,846] worth of merchandise and luxury automobiles. Information developed during the course of this investigation contributed to the development of a secondary investigation that resulted in the seizure of an additional approximately 2.1 million MDMA tablets at the Los Angeles International Airport on 22 July 2000.*

On the same day that Britney Chambers died (see p146), a 24-year-old Hollander was charged with attempting to smuggle $70,000 (£50,000) worth of ecstasy into Miami. He had swallowed 3,500 pills, boarded a plane in Amsterdam and was apprehended by customs officials at Miami International Airport.

DEEP BLUE E

There is still a place for the romantic notion of smuggling – that involving ships, sea voyages and clandestine bays once land has been accurately announced as 'Ahoy'. It's not a big place, as yet, but law enforcers expect it to get bigger as wholesale organizations become more sophisticated. There have been reports of maritime MDMA smuggling from Europe to Florida and the Caribbean, and also to New York via Montreal, and the trend will likely increase when traffickers realise the main advantage of maritime smuggling over mail smuggling – quantity. You can fit considerably more ecstasy tablets inside a small cargo hold than even the biggest and most intricate of jigsaw puzzles.

AIRFREIGHT SHIPMENTS

As above, but with wings.

OVERLAND

This is a new method catering for the recent influx of Mexican ecstasy traffickers offering healthy competition to the Europeans and Israelis. MDMA is transported across the southwestern US border in private motor vehicles or even by motorcycle gangs.

GOOD E TWO SHOES

Ecstasy has a good reputation. That may seem a contradiction in the light of the Betts, Spinks, Kirkland and Chambers cases (see Chapter 5), but relatively speaking it is very much the case. Compared to cocaine and (especially) heroin, MDMA is a positively benevolent drug in the eyes of the traffickers, who have minor interest in the benignity of the drugs they shift but major interest in the consequences should they get caught doing so.

They reckon that MDMA is safer to transport in two respects: customs officials are less vigilant with it than they are with the genuinely addictive cocaine and heroin; and punishments will be less severe if their operatives are caught.

Consequently many criminal gangs with access to weapons and no compunction about hurting people have switched entirely to the domain of MDMA dealing, where they have little to fear from the occasional middle-class entrepreneur with PLUR ideals.

MONOPOLY DISCORD

This increased competition has caused the breaking up of the original Holland/Belgium MDMA monopoly, with various Central American, eastern European and Middle Eastern DTOs getting in on this new and thriving market. There has therefore opened a competitive global MDMA market, with the usual dramatic results:

- Dramatic increase in produce;
- Dramatic decrease in price;
- Dramatic fall-off in quality.

There is an increasing involvement of non-European MDMA DTOs that includes those from the Dominican Republic, Asia, Colombia and (especially) Mexico, where MDMA is both produced and distributed for US consumption. In July 2001, the United States Customs Service (USCS) seized 55,000 MDMA pills smuggled into the US at Brownsville. This is the largest shipment ever seized along the US-Mexico border. In this instance, a private vehicle was being driven by Dominican nationals setting off from Mexico City.

ASIAN TAKEAWAY

MDMA has also been identified in Asia and Southeast Asia - in countries like Burma and Thailand. Also, two MDMA laboratories were recently seized in China, indicating that some DTOs operate there. Current evidence, however, suggests that this Chinese takeaway service is only a small-fry operation.

On top of this, some old-style DTOs have dealt the fuck-off pill to capitalism and abandoned money in favour of some mutually helpful swapping: trading kilogrammes of cocaine for tablets of MDMA. In one instance the DEA observed one 1kg (2¼lb) of cocaine being traded in Spain for around 13,000 MDMA pills, and then smuggled back to the US.

MIDDLE EASTERN PROMISE

Israel is another boarder of the happy MDMA bandwagon.

- There are reports of Hell's Angels allying with Israelis to smuggle MDMA across the US-Canada border.
- In two recent cases Israelis were arrested in New York with 600,000 MDMA pills.
- US, Mexican and American groups have allied with Israeli and Russian criminal groups, who source their MDMA from Europe.
- Drugs from ethnic sources have been found as far apart as Chicago, Houston, Miami, New Orleans and San Francisco.

THE EUROPEAN MARKET

Within Europe the MDMA trade is held firmly in the hot mitts of organized crime, and had been for some time. More recently, though, the aforementioned Israeli/Russian partnerships moved into a particularly significant patch of European territory. Former eastern bloc countries are celebrating their embracement of the free market with, for example, Polish gangs trafficking both the precursor chemicals and the finished drug both within the motherland and abroad. Spain and the Iberian Peninsula are surfacing as ideal shipment areas for MDMA leaving Europe. There have been some incidents indicating that Dutch and Colombian traffickers have bartered ecstasy for cocaine in Spain – in July 2000, four individuals (two Dutch and two Colombian) were arrested by Spanish authorities for possession of large amounts of ecstasy and cocaine.

E-TAIL OUTLETS

Getting the ecstasy past customs is just the beginning of it. Once the courier, the Fed Ex man or the salt has done their bit, the drugs are picked up by mid-level wholesale distributors to pass on to retail distribution groups or individual dealers. Quite what constitutes 'mid' is indeterminate, however. These mid-level wholesalers are supplied with anything between 1,000 and 500,000 pills at a time. Indeed the trend is toward larger operations at mid-level. Other drugs – heroin and cocaine, in particular – usually pass through far more levels at retail distribution or individual levels, because at each level the drugs are further adulterated (or 'cut') to increase profit. With a drug like MDMA, where pills are pressed in the source labs, this is not an issue. MDMA smuggled in by methods other than express mail (where it is picked up direct by the dealers) is sent to stash sites in a hub city. US-based distributors are reasonably proficient at their job – they have worked out strategies, drawn up rosters and established an element of continuity and consistency to their distribution patterns. They tend to receive their tablets in relatively small doses of 1,000 to 2,000 pills, and stagger nightclubs to ply their narcotic wares at the same venues on specific nights.

The head of the US Drug Enforcement Administration, Asa Hutchinson, told delegates at an international anti-drug conference in Bolivia in March 2002 that use of ecstasy was growing because of a misconception among the young that the drug is harmless.

COUNTER STRATEGIES

The primary tactic employed by American law enforcers to counter the DTOs is to concentrate on the mid-level wholesale and retail levels. These seem to lack the guile of their heroin and cocaine counterparts and sell to unfamiliar and new customers in obvious places – like rave clubs and university campuses – leaving them vulnerable to the hoary old police tactic of sending in an undercover cop to score some gear. Information obtained from these 'buy-bust' operations can then be collated for use in bigger investigations.

It is more difficult to address the smuggling process itself because if US law enforcers manage temporarily to control one avenue, such as federal mail delivery, DTOs just shift the smuggling to another mode like maritime. As ever, the judiciary is stepping in to help, by proposing an increase of federal penalties for MDMA trafficking to bring them into line with those for methamphetamines - to remove, in other words, MDMA's good name.

CONSUMPTION TRENDS

Ecstasy is no longer just a club drug. Increasingly it is being sold in more diverse places such as schools, private homes and on the streets. These trends have increased the MDMA user base no end. This is excellent news for the competing trafficking cartels.

INFORMATION COLLATED FROM US SURVEY GROUPS

MONITORING THE FUTURE (MTM)

This survey was conducted in 2000 to discover drug-taking tendencies in US adolescents:

- From 1999 to 2000, MDMA use increased among the three grade levels measured in the study - eighth, tenth and twelfth. This is the second consecutive year MDMA use has increased.
- MDMA use increased among eighth graders from 1.7 per cent in 1999 to 3.1 per cent in 2000, from 4.4 per cent to 5.4 per cent among tenth graders, and from 5.6 per cent to 8.2 per cent among twelfth graders. Also among twelfth graders, the perceived availability of MDMA rose from 40.1 per cent in 1999 to 51.4 per cent in 2000.
- African-American students showed lesser rates of ecstasy use than white or Hispanic students.

DEA AND THE US CUSTOMS SERVICE (USCS)

- During 2000, around 6.4 million people over 12 years old had tried MDMA at least once in their lifetime: an increase from 5.1 million the previous year.
- Arrests for MDMA violations increased from 681 in 1999 to 1,456 in 2000.
- The number of DEA cases initiated against MDMA traffickers jumped from 278 to 670 during the same period.

- MDMA seizures by DEA and USCS have increased every year since 1988.

COMMUNITY EPIDEMIOLOGY WORK GROUP (CEWG)

- MDMA is now being used in other social settings beyond raves and campuses.
- MDMA is the most prominent narcotic used in Chicago; sold in singles bars in Denver; used by a wide variety of people and in a wide variety of places in Atlanta; and is the middle-class drug of the moment in Washington, DC.
- In 1999 there were eight MDMA-related deaths in Miami, and five in Minneapolis/St Paul.
- In Boston during January to September 2000, MDMA was the most frequent subject of calls to the Poison Control Center.
- Snorting of MDMA has been reported in Atlanta and Chicago, as has injecting in Atlanta, and rectal insertion in Chicago.
- Ecstasy frequently consists of substances entirely different from MDMA.
- MDMA is increasingly mixed with marijuana.
- Ecstasy tablets seized by the DEA increased from 13,342 in 1996 to 949,257 in 2000.

NATIONAL HOUSEHOLD SURVEY ON DRUG ABUSE (NHSDA)

Each year, NHSDA reports on the nature and extent of drug use among the American household population aged 12 and older. The 1998 survey is the latest for data relating to MDMA use.

- About 1.5 per cent (3.4 million) of Americans had used MDMA at least once during their lifetime.
- By age group, the heaviest use (5 per cent or 1.4 million people) was reported as those between 18 and 25 years of age.

POPULARIT-E

There have been reports of massively increased referrals to US emergency rooms (casualty departments) during the last six years that has corresponded with an equivalent increase in MDMA seizure. This suggests that MDMA is still growing in popularity. Greatly increased emergency-room reports over the past six years, as well as a corresponding increase in MDMA pill seizures over the same period, strongly indicate that MDMA is still growing in popularity. If current trends are maintained, it is predicted that the US MDMA incidence will approach that of methamphetamine by 2003.

E-QUIVALENT TRENDS IN THE UK

The United Kingdom mirrors the US in sterling fashion.

- Medium-level dealers can sell bags of 50 Es for less than £200 ($290).
- The street price of E has dropped from around £25 ($35) in the mid-1990s to as little as £2 ($3) in some northeastern towns.
- As in the US, E has moved from a drug exclusively associated with raves to one that has spread to bars, colleges, high schools and even junior high schools (junior schools).

FOREIGN BODIES

In accordance with the greater competition between rival MDMA traffickers, recent years have seen a change in the sociological makeup of the mid- and low-level ecstasy dealers. As mentioned earlier, the mid-level retail of E originally involved independent entrepreneurial Caucasians carrying out their work with a hint of genuine benevolence to complement their self-centred moneymaking schemes. Now they've got competition.

Over the past two years there has been a more widespread distribution involving more dealers from ethnic backgrounds, including Mexicans, Colombians, Dominicans, African Americans, Arabs, Vietnamese, Chinese, Hungarians and Romanians.

It is, after all, a very profitable and expanding business and retail distributors need little incentive to sign up for it. Each MDMA pill sold at the retail level can earn the dealer £7-21 ($10-30) in profits. Individual distributors say that they can sell as many as 1,000 pills a night at clubs because many users buy several pills during one night.

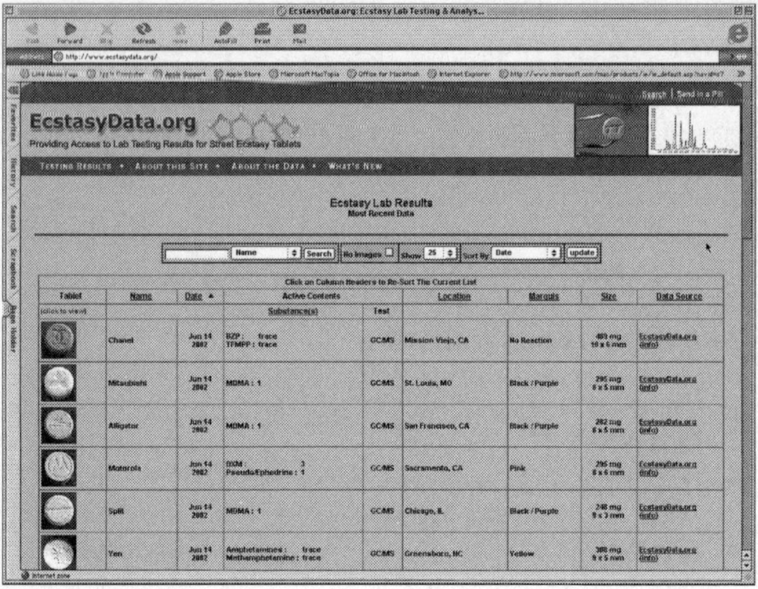
EcstasyData.org

Providing Access to Lab Testing Results for Street Ecstasy Tablets

TESTING RESULTS • ABOUT THIS SITE • ABOUT THE DATA • WHAT'S NEW

Ecstasy Lab Results

Most Recent Data

Click on Column Headers to Re-Sort The Current List

Tablet	Name	Date ▲	Active Contents		Location	Marquis	Size	Data Source
(click to view)			Substance(s)	Test				
	Chanel	Jun 14 2002	BZP: trace TFMPP: trace	GC/MS	Mission Viejo, CA	No Reaction	469 mg 10 x 6 mm	EcstasyData.org (info)
	Mitsubishi	Jun 14 2002	MDMA: 1	GC/MS	St. Louis, MO	Black / Purple	295 mg 8 x 5 mm	EcstasyData.org (info)
	Alligator	Jun 14 2002	MDMA: 1	GC/MS	San Francisco, CA	Black / Purple	282 mg 8 x 5 mm	EcstasyData.org (info)
	Motorola	Jun 14 2002	DXM: 3 Pseudo/Ephedrine: 1	GC/MS	Sacramento, CA	Pink	295 mg 8 x 6 mm	EcstasyData.org (info)
	Split	Jun 14 2002	MDMA: 1	GC/MS	Chicago, IL	Black / Purple	248 mg 9 x 3 mm	EcstasyData.org (info)
	Yen	Jun 14 2002	Amphetamines: trace Methamphetamine: trace	GC/MS	Greensboro, NC	Yellow	308 mg 9 x 5 mm	EcstasyData.org (info)

Pages from website www.ecstasydata.org which provides acsess to lab testing results for street ecstasy tablets. Constantly updated, the data includes over 900 entries, listed over 37 pages.

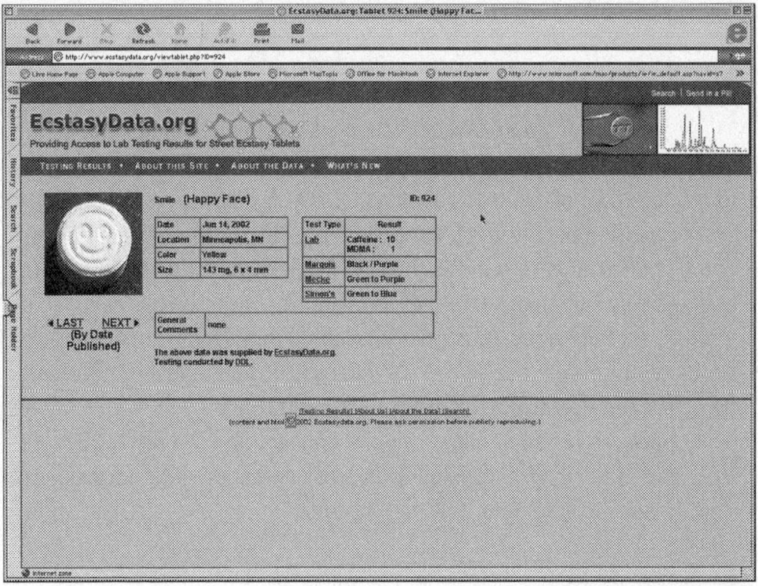
EcstasyData.org: Tablet 924: Smile (Happy Fac...
Back
Forward
Refresh
Print
Mail
http://www.ecstasydata.org/viewtablet.php?ID=924
Search | Send in a Pill
EcstasyData.org
Providing Access to Lab Testing Results for Street Ecstasy Tablets
TESTING RESULTS • ABOUT THIS SITE • ABOUT THE DATA • WHAT'S NEW
Smile (Happy Face)
ID: 924
Date Jun 14, 2002
Location Minneapolis, MN
Color Yellow
Size 143 mg, 6 x 4 mm
Test Type Result
Lab Caffeine: 10 MDMA: 1
Marquis Black / Purple
Mecke Green to Purple
Simon's Green to Blue
LAST NEXT
(By Date Published)
General Comments none
The above data was supplied by EcstasyData.org.
Testing conducted by DDL.
Internet zone

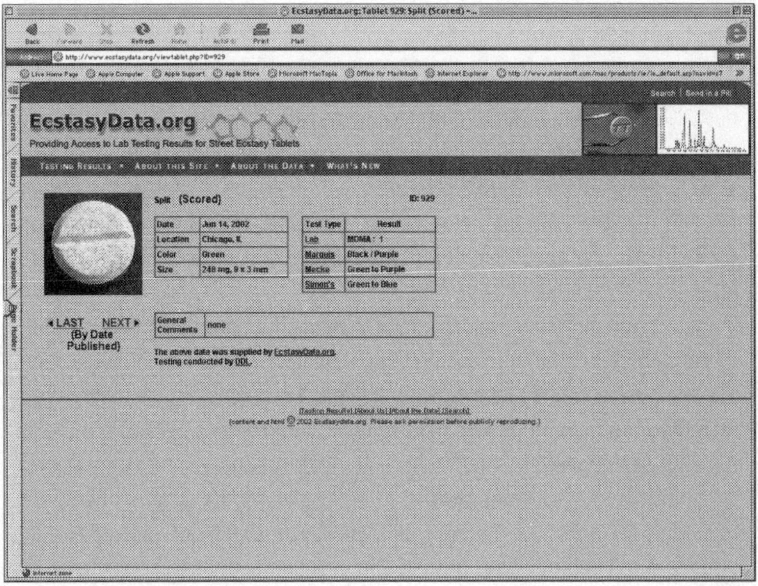
EcstasyData.org: Tablet 929: Split (Scored) -...
Back
Refresh
Print
Mail
http://www.ecstasydata.org/viewtablet.php?ID=929
Search | Send in a Pill
EcstasyData.org
Providing Access to Lab Testing Results for Street Ecstasy Tablets
TESTING RESULTS • ABOUT THIS SITE • ABOUT THE DATA • WHAT'S NEW
Split (Scored)
ID: 929
Date Jun 14, 2002
Location Chicago, IL
Color Green
Size 248 mg, 9 x 3 mm
Test Type Result
Lab MDMA: 1
Marquis Black / Purple
Mecke Green to Purple
Simon's Green to Blue
LAST NEXT
(By Date Published)
General Comments none
The above data was supplied by EcstasyData.org.
Testing conducted by DDL.
Internet zone

WORLD WAR E

The happy atmosphere in the field of ecstasy dealing has been comprehensively blown to buggery by this new intake of traffickers. Replacing the amiable fellows selling MDMA to their mates, partly for a small profit but mainly just for sheer generosity, are the worst elements of the criminal underground aggressively competing for profits. At street level the distribution of MDMA now involves established drugs gangs that formerly shifted heroin and cocaine – including Chinese, African Americans, Arabs, Vietnamese, Canadians, Dominicans, Colombians, Hungarians, Mexicans and Romanian – all at each other's throats.

Consequently, something previously unheard of in the ecstasy culture is coming to carry the same significance as glowsticks – internecine gang warfare and violent crime. This has included:

- MDMA involved in the murder of rival gangs;
- Shootouts with police in New York City and Detroit;
- Weapons seized with MDMA at street level.

It was violence that marked the end of the UK 'Madchester' scene in the early 1990s. The lead singer with The Stone Roses, Ian Brown, who actually saw a gang leader get shot at a reggae concert, said at the time, '[There was] a feeling of community strength...coming out of a club at the end of the night feeling like you were going to change the world. Then guns come in, and heroin starts being put in ecstasy. It took a lot of the love-vibe out.'

A veteran of the rave scene wrote to me of the hardened drugs dealers at the periphery of the ecstasy market: 'I have one friend, who often supplies us, who flirts with serious dealers. He always wants to move up into the "big time", but sadly his gullibility and latent generosity make him one of the worst dealers known to mankind. However, his connections do mean we got to meet people living on the very margins of society (including the infamous 'Souperman', who, because he is of no fixed abode, you have to keep out of your house in case he decides to stay with you, boring you with his tales of how to hide pills and launder money). Many of the people my friend knows ended up in prison or hooked on heroin, but to me they have never been anything to do with the rave scene. They would live and die that life-style regardless of what music or drugs are in fashion.'

DOUBLE E-DGED SWORD

Internet technology, as is well-known, is a two faced beast with (for example) the wonder of real-time global communication being blunted by the activity of predatory paedophiles in chatrooms, and the revolution of electronic mail being sometimes ground to a halt by the accretion of junk posts from Korea.

A third, two-faced, facet has recently come to the attention of law enforcers. The Internet has become a haven for mail-order shopping, where the lack of the high-street stores' overheads allows retailers to be unprecedentedly competitive. The flip side of this is that drugs retailers can do exactly the same thing.

In March 2002, *Globalization And New Technologies*, a report from the International Narcotics Control Board (INCB), informed about the aforementioned Internet 'recipe' sites and other increasingly technological methods used by DTOs to further their trade, such as touting through chatrooms and storing on computers encrypted details of law enforcers' bank details and even grid coordinates of landing strips'. They use their great wealth to recruit bent hackers with enough expertise to keep the DTOs several steps ahead of the law. The report added that some Internet techniques only came to light after law enforcers interviewed 30 American and Colombian suspected drug smugglers. These included:

- DTO-run chatrooms protected by impenetrable firewalls;
- Hugely sophisticated encryption technology;
- Host computers situated on ships outside of US jurisdiction;
- Personal information on DEA investigators collected by criminal computer hackers;
- Details of freight consignments altered through hacking into customs databases;

- Diversionary websites, which are deliberately difficult to hack into and therefore waste law enforcers' time;
- Laundering money quickly via global money markets, online casinos and Internet banking services.

The gist of *Globalization And New Technologies* is that too little coordinated attempt is being made to put a stop to this, especially from countries outside of the US, UK and Japan – which are therefore becoming 'data havens' for DTOs' online operations.

MY DUTY-FREE LAUNDERETTE

Ecstasy DTOs have proved rather adept at concealing the influx of money back to Europe. Law enforcers still don't know how they do it, although investigations turned up some investment in real-estate and US business.

THOU SHALT COMMIT ADULTERY

The increasing number of global trafficking organizations, and the consequent profit motive taking over from the ravers' PLUR ideals, has heralded an accordant increase in the number of impure MDMA tablets in the guise of 'ecstasy'. It is important to emphasize that there are two categories of 'impure' ecstasy pill:

- Those that are deliberately adulterated with other substances, and are knowingly taken as such by druggies who like to mix and match. (See 'A Brief Guide To E' on pp54–5.)
- Those that are, without the consumers' knowledge, mixed with any old shit to make up the volume.

It is the second category that is relevant here. Recently, MDMA traffickers have begun to deal in Es that are of necessity adulterated in the source laboratories where the pills are pressed. This particularly takes place in the non-European labs – like those in Mexico and the Dominican Republic – and can take the form of tablets that forge 'reputable' ecstasy brands.

Examples are the following, although this is really just skimming the chemical surface:

- Yin-yang pills containing only MDE (3,4-methylenedioxyethylamphetamine, a more hallucinogenic analogue of MDMA);
- Green-triangle pills containing only DXM (dextromethorphan, a drug that can cause audio hallucinations);
- Wild-flower pills containing MDA only;
- Mitsubishi, containing caffeine only (in other words, glorified Pro-Plus pills).

Users who had taken these pills reported nausea, delirium, itchy skin, loss of motor control, and audio and visual hallucinations.

TRAFFIC SCRAM

The trafficking and distribution of MDMA is increasingly becoming like that of heroin and cocaine, with the worst elements of the criminal underground in fierce competition with each other. The consequence is gang violence and increasingly adulterated MDMA. This is a very worrying trend, and there is seemingly no end to it. This is very far from the original purpose of MDMA, and must cause those who pioneered it as a therapeutic aid to roll in their graves or shake their chemical-stained fists in anger (as applicable). To learn more of these people, we must look at the history of the drug MDMA.

03 HISTORY

> 'MDMA is penicillin for the soul, and you don't give up prescribing penicillin, once you've seen what it can do.'
>
> – Alexander Shulgin

BRIEF E-NCOUNTER

This history of ecstasy is necessarily brief. Stephen Hawking came to the same conclusion with his *A Brief History Of Time*, though for different reasons. Hawking had to compact his history because time, as Douglas Adams could have written, is too 'damn big' for him to do otherwise. The history of ecstasy is the exact opposite. It is too damn small. Compared to other drugs covered in this series, ecstasy is the smallest of spring chickens – in fact, it would make a quail look ungainly by comparison.

SCORING A CENTURY

Ecstasy under its current street-name, when used as a dance drug, dates back no further than 20 years. Before that, under its real and decidedly less snappy name of '3,4 methylenedioxynmethylamphetamine' (MDMA), it appears for around 40 years either in the labs of experimental psychotherapists or else being fed to guinea pigs – both actual ones and those perennial metaphorical ones, the armed forces. During the 30 years following its patent, it just sat on its backside and put its feet up all day.

Around 90 years old, then – give or take an insignificant decade or two – which is frankly nothing when put alongside the millennium-spanning annals of recorded alcohol and cannabis use. The history of ecstasy is a mere cat's eye on the freeway of narcotic substances.

JUVENILE E-LINQUENT

This is not to say that the history of ecstasy is short of incident. Far from it. The youthful MDMA grew up in America as a sensitive and sensible teenager, albeit one with an imaginative turn of mind. It was not until its college days that upstart tendencies developed. MDMA took on the nickname of 'adam' before choosing another moniker that carried far more street credibility.

The newly named 'ecstasy' took a gap year and toured the world: it digested a guru's mysticism in India; gave rhythm and stole serenity from the resort of Ibiza, becoming just the latest in a millennium-spanning sequence of cultural invaders descending on that Spanish island (admittedly, most of the earlier ones had worn moustaches and brought venereal disease with them); raved in British barn houses; revitalized the Manchester and London club scenes; and finally returned to the homeland, where it shared its experiences with a new generation of San Franciscan college students.

Now ecstasy is reluctantly approaching adulthood. It is losing the exuberance of youth, has become somewhat blemished in reputation and it has an uncertain future.

BLAME THE PARENT

MDA, the parent drug of the MDA group of drugs that includes MDMA, was synthesized by two German scientists in 1910. Quite what these men had in mind when they devised the drug is uncertain; it was certainly not the subject of human research. Possibly MDA was intended as a medium pharmaceutical for the preparation of other chemicals, rather than something specifically therapeutic or recreational. The distinction is blurred, because at the time there was less of a cultural schism between recreational and therapeutic drugs; then, you could happily mosey to your local pharmacy and pick up a pack of aspirin, a tincture of cocaine and a reusable prophylactic for the weekend (and any number of subsequent weekends).

THE GERMAN(E) E CREATORS

MDMA itself was probably first synthesized by Merck Pharmaceuticals, a German company, who attempted to synthesize a medicine called hydrastinine, and discovered MDMA as an unexpected by-product. This was duly patented in 1914.

THE SHIT AND POLISH ONES

I say 'probably' above because there is a source that steadfastly insists that MDMA was first synthesized by two Polish chemists, S Biniecki and E Krajewski, as late as 1960. Although this argument goes against such irrelevances as clear documentation to the contrary (the patent itself, MDMA's 1950s listing as 'Experimental Agent 1229' and so on), it is unfair to dismiss it as (to use a technical term) arrant bollocks without hearing it out. No doubt there is perfectly valid evidence to support this contention, involving such factors as pedantic differences between formulae and more exacting methods of production...and the use of a TARDIS.

COROLLARY ATTACK

Assuming that Merck did indeed synthesize and patent MDMA, then counter to (very relative) popular myth, they never considered it as an appetite suppressant. That happened later.

Again, assuming that Merck did first patent MDMA, it has a lot to answer for.

DELAYED E-FFECT

Like the plays of Chekhov, the poetry of Blake, the songs of Schubert, the symphonies of Mahler and the fine exemplars of sub-Wildean comedy called *Carry On* films, the drug MDMA was not an initial success and lay in a pool of near oblivion for nearly 30 years.

TEST-E-ALITY

Around 1939, MDMA dared sneak its pecker up above the near-oblivion-pool's, only to be hauled out for use as an experimental substance into studies of adrenaline. This was the first time lucky animals were the beneficiaries of MDMA's euphoric and life-affirming effects before having their brains scalpelled open (see pp128–9). Seeing as the effect of adrenaline on the animal kingdom is generally irrelevant to humans – the beasts of the field are not often obliged to take exams or give public speeches – these tests were not continued for long, and MDMA pulled its pecker back below the murky surface for a couple more years.

FAT LOT OF USE

In 1941, US pharmacists dropped plans to market MDMA as an appetite suppressant because of its unpalatable side effects. They perhaps realised that it was a terrible waste of resources to cause obese people to feel empathic toward one another when it would be far funnier to give them amphetamine instead and have them all running around pretending to be aeroplanes.

NO GREAT SHAKES

Also in 1941, doctors tested MDMA as a relief for Parkinson's disease but they soon rejected it when one trial subject experienced increased rigidity. To a layperson such as myself, that would appear to be the point, but I presume that the dedicated wartime medics knew what they were up to.

THE MILITARY MIND

A decade-long MDMA moratorium followed until 1953/1954, when the CIA and the army tested it on the US military – sometimes without the subjects' knowledge – as part of a series of drugs experiments looking (bizarrely, in retrospect) into:

- chemical warfare;
- the extraction of information from prisoners;
- immobilization of enemy troops.

It proved to be useless for these purposes. Accordingly, MDMA was coded 'EA1299' by scientists at the ECWS, though rumours that carried the tag 'No Fucking Use Whatsoever' (NFUW) were unfounded. Everyone forgot about MDMA (except, one presumes, relatives of the psychiatric subject who died following an intravenous injection of 500mg).

SPREAD THE GOOD NEWS

Any prospective drug needs its messiah to preach its Sermon on the Mount. In the case of MDMA, the messiah was (and still is) a remarkable chemist called Alexander Shulgin. But more on him later.

Every good messiah in his turn needs a John the Baptist. Shulgin's John the Baptist was a US researcher called Gordon Alles, though the original one had his head done in more permanently. Alles was to MDMA what Albert Hoffman was to LSD: he synthesized it, dropped it, then spread the good news far and wide. In 1957, Alles described MDMA's effects of heightened perception and visual imagery to a scientific meeting, thus setting off the chain of events that would bring the effects of MDMA to the attention of Alexander Shulgin some ten years later.

MESSIAH

If Alles was to MDMA what Hoffman was to LSD, then Shulgin is MDMA's counterpart to Aldous Huxley or Timothy Leary. There are, though, notable differences. While Shulgin happily continues the latter's policies of turning on and tuning in, he falls somewhat short of the mark when it comes to dropping out.

'ON YOUR PSYCH, SONNY'

The earliest part of Shulgin's life that matters is his research work at the Dow Chemical Company during the 1950s. The thing about reputable chemical concerns is that they like their chemicals, and by extension the chemists that synthesize them, to enhance their reputation, not denigrate it. Shulgin characteristically drew a line and rolled up a greenback at such pleasantries. Chemistry was not only his job but also very much his hobby. In his free time, he would use company-owned agents and facilities to create all manner of mind-expanding substances, and in due course went one-step too far: he committed the heinous crime of being caught at it. Once the Dow Chemical Company was discovered in possession of the formulae for several prohibited substances, and the miscellany was traced back to one of the laboratory staff, Shulgin was told to clear his nose and leave.

SINGLE, GOING STEAD-E

Just as well that, like Cliff Richard, Shulgin worked best as a solo artist. He continued the good work in his own time.

Shulgin's interesting drugs philosophy effectively bypassed the health arguments, both physical and psychological, that gather around substance use like moths around an electric insect killer. It applied to both addictive and non/unknown addictive substances and also the whole gamut of drug seriousness: from soft delicacies like hashish and Benylin, through hard nuts like smack and cocaine through to known killers like tobacco and diesel oil. It was really a very simple five-word philosophy: he didn't give a shit (he may have taken it, but he didn't give it).

Shulgin himself put it a tad more eloquently: 'I personally have chosen some drugs to be of sufficient value to be worth the risks; others, I deem not to be of sufficient value... I used to [smoke tobacco] quite heavily, then gave it up. It was not the health risk that swayed me, but rather the fact that I had become completely dependent on it.' Shulgin believed that, with hallucinogens, the potential for learning far outweighed the risks inherent in the drug. He saw no moral distinction between prohibited drugs like pot and heroin, and everyday substances like caffeine. His take on heroin, for example, was that 'I have tried heroin. This drug of course is one of the major concerns in our society, at the present time. In me, it produces a dreamy peacefulness, with no rough edges of worry, stress or concern. But there is also a loss of motivation, of alertness, and the urge to get things done. It is not any fear of addiction that causes me to decide against heroin; it is the fact that, under its influence, nothing seems to be particularly important to me.'

POLITICAL E-ATURE

Shulgin took a political stance that coming from others might seem like conspiracist paranoia, but coming from the ironically very level-headed Shulgin seemed nothing more than fair comment. His gist was that current Western governments, as opposed to some Eastern ones and European ones of past, have a vested interest in limiting free thinking and therefore individual liberties; and that the study of states of mind is the ultimate in free thinking. Governments restrict free thinking via a mixture of paternalism (whereby they provide for their citizens' needs in return for them doing exactly what they are told) and provincialism (whereby local bigotry and fear of the unknown is tacitly encouraged until such free thinking becomes the act of a pariah).

TRAD-E TEST TRANSMISSIONS

In a hallucinogenic sense, Shulgin followed the same work routine as the newspaper entertainments critic or the lazier sort of housewife – he sat at home watching television all day. However, this particular television was not the sort that comes with surround-sound speakers and an unfeasibly multi-buttoned remote control unit. Shulgin's television was built into his person. In this respect, he was the original Tellytubby.

What Shulgin likened to a television is the unconscious mind, that favourite frontier land of hypnotists and spiritualists. In lieu of the remote control unit, he used variously psychedelic drugs, most of which he synthesized himself, to 'change channels', to explore different facets of his unconscious mind.

There is a crucial aspect to Shulgin's philosophy, one that might royally piss off ravers were they to attempt to cite him as a guru. Drug experiences are only of value *if something is learned*. They want to address their inadequacies, not escape them. Taking a drug for its own sake or for instant highs is of *no value whatsoever*. The obvious corollary is that dropping a combination of MDMA and dog-worming pills for the sole purpose of dancing all night and hugging strangers is outside any responsible researcher's brief.

ANIMAL CRACKERS

Red squirrel monkeys and rats were safe from Shulgin (see Chapter 4 for accounts of MDMA experiments on animals). He had no use for animal research, not for any misguided 'animal rights' reason but because they indeed *were* of no use to him. The lanes and alleys that twist around, say, cats' unconscious minds had no relevance to Shulgin's research because their brains are the size of walnuts and their vocabulary of miaows, hisses and purrs were not the ideal medium for an in-depth documentation of neurological experience.

THERE'S NO SHAMAN IN IT

Shulgin cited the shaman of Native American and other aboriginal groups as his exemplar. Like the shaman, Shulgin's policy was straightforward - he took the drugs and saw what happened...only somewhat more systematically.

INCREMENTS AND SENSIBILITY

Shulgin took newly synthesized drugs in gradually increasing increments, with a day's break in between to avoid developing a tolerance. Once he regained contact with planet Earth, he recorded his findings using the following system of plus and minus signs, the scores on perception's doors, so to speak:

(-) No effect noted that can be ascribed to the drug in question - 'baseline' ie 'normal state';

(+-) a move off 'baseline' but not necessarily a drug effect - possibly a 'false positive';

(+) a real effect whose duration can be tracked but whose nature can't be categorized;

(++) an unmistakable drug effect - not only can its duration be perceived, but also so can its nature;

(+++) a maximum intensity of drug effect - the full potential of the drug has been realised, its character can be fully appreciated (assuming that amnesia was not one of its properties), and it is possible to exactly define its chronological pattern;

(++++) a separate category in a class by itself, not comparable to (+++); a serene and magical state largely independent of what drug is used.

SHULGIN IN THE 1960s

Reckoning that two's a marriage but three's a drugs party, Shulgin invited a select group of scientists and psychologist friends to join him and his wife in an ongoing sequence of psychedelic sleepovers (RSVP, and bring a bong). Realising that the act of consuming virgin psychedelics is the very definition of 'unpredictable', a set of house rules were of necessity set up. These included the following:

- Any one of the group could have absolute veto over the drugs taken, and the conditions under which they were to be taken;
- People were not to have drug-induced sex with non-partners, however unprecedentedly and devastatingly attractive they suddenly found the hitherto unassuming person sitting opposite to be;
- If, however, they wished to make psychedelic whoopee with their usual spouse or partner, then the gist was 'Be our guest – the bedrooms are upstairs and we promise not to listen.'

At the time of publication of his autobiography, *PiHKAL: A Chemical Love Story* (Transform Press, 1991), Shulgin had settled on steady groups of 11 friends with whom to experiment.

REBEL WITHOUT APPLAUSE

Shulgin is a remarkable figure in that he combined the out-and-out subversion of a Timothy Leary with the eloquence and anti-didactic non-confrontationalism of a Mahatma Gandhi. It is very hard to argue with someone who will not have it out back at you. Consequently, he has much influential respect in the US, which allowed him sufficient funds to carry his research into the present day with the full backing of the US government.

COMETH THE MDMA, COMETH THE MAN

Alexander Shulgin, of course, did not himself originally synthesize MDMA. That was the handiwork of the aforementioned Merck Pharmaceuticals, or alternatively the two Polish travellers through the dimensions of space and time.

Shulgin happened upon MDMA by chance in 1967, though it is fairly certain that he would eventually have found it in any case. He was working at the University of California in San Francisco when a graduate student invited him to try the drug (things were a tad less formal between teachers and pupils in those days).

To say that Shulgin was impressed would be a gross understatement. It is fair to say that he raved about it, though certainly not in the modern sense of the word. Shulgin describes the psychological effect as 'like a window: not psychedelic in the visual or interpretive sense but the lightness and warmth of psychedelics was present and quite remarkable'. He further adds: 'I was suddenly one with myself, one with the world; I was a person who had no secrets from himself and one who could trust others to be as honest with him as he was with himself.'

Shulgin took to embarrassing people on trains by discarding the Martini from its glass and replacing it with his own cocktail of MDMA and quinine (whether he put the olive back in is unknown). He described the drug as 'penicillin for the soul' and maintained that it could be all things to all people. He claims that he cured one man of bad LSD flashbacks, and cured another man - a stutterer - so successfully that he went too far the other way and became a speech therapist.

THE ROAD TO ADAMASCUS

If Alles was John the Baptist and Shulgin was the Messiah, then 'Leo' was St Paul. 'Leo' was an ageing psychologist with a reprobate streak: he would illegally and clandestinely use psychedelics to explore the unconscious minds of his clients. It is hardly surprising, therefore, that Alexander Shulgin was, to put it mildly, a good mate of 'Leo''s.

Shulgin visited 'Leo' with a little present in tow: a certain four-lettered psychedelic/amphetamine hybrid that 'Leo' (with his dedication for all things hallucinogenic) might find of interest. He certainly did. After 'Leo' retired as a therapist, he worked harder than ever as an evangelist. He toured the US introducing MDMA to other therapists, until congregations of professional MDMA disciples met all over the continent.

STREET SCENE

By the late 1960s, knowledge of MDMA and its analogues was spreading via various sources. These included the motion started by Gordon Alles after the aforementioned 1957 meeting, as well as that begun by Shulgin, and preached via 'Leo' (the latter one mainly reaching professionals and therapists). Whatever the source, people were aware of MDMA.

It was, however, the parent drug MDA that first hit the streets of America's West Coast in 1968. Here it was known as 'the love drug', and presumably induced hippies whose throats were too dry from pulling on bongs to group-hug and tickle each other's jet-black feet via a toke substitute in tablet form.

The government eventually took umbrage to this – as governments tend to do when young people are harmlessly enjoying themselves – and controlled MDA under US drug law in 1970. The hippies' response was immediate (this is a definition of 'immediate' that takes into account the time-slowing qualities of psychedelic trips). In 1972, canny dopeheads introduced a 'designer drug' to the streets of San Francisco.

In 2001, the Food and Drug Administration (FDA), which regulates the licensing and testing of pharmaceutical products in the US, astonished the research community by approving a double-blind clinical trial of MDMA to treat post-traumatic stress disorder (PTSD).

A designer drug is a substance that carries similar effects to a listed illegal drug, but has been synthesized to evade the law. This 'new' drug, MDMA, soon became a students' recreational drug and, later in the Reagan years, the yuppies' substance of choice.

DRUGGISTS' THERAPY

Simultaneously US psychologists, who had discovered MDMA via the 'Leo' route, were using the drug – which they now called 'adam' – in several ways, most significantly as a marriage-guidance drug. (One of MDMA's less documented features is that it inhibits urges to hurl teacups and shred a husband's shirts with scissors.) The ever-neutral Swiss still use it in this way.

These therapists continually worried that their wonder drug would (as did LSD) emerge as a popular street drug and become outlawed by the US government. They were damn right to worry.

On 27 July 1984, the DEA announced that it was adding MDMA to the list of Schedule I substances (the sort that carries the most stringent penalties for dealers or users). It claimed that MDMA had no legitimate medical use and was responsible for an undisclosed number of hospitalizations. This was one of the most counterproductive moves ever: it rocketed a hitherto minority drug to overnight stardom.

GREER PRESSURE

One MDMA practitioner, psychiatrist Dr George Greer, reckoned that if he synthesized the drug himself, and obtained their informed consent, he could legally administer it to his patients. Aided by Shulgin, he manufactured a batch of MDMA and gave it to around 80 patients over five years. Over nine out of ten patients reported significant benefits, including the following:

- Improvement of communication and intimacy with spouses;
- General decrease in psychological problems;
- Improvements in interpersonal relationships, self-esteem and mood.

Some patients reported these as long-term (years, even) improvements, even after only one or two MDMA sessions.

Greer and 15 other medical professionals petitioned the DEA, explaining that in their own first-hand professional experiences MDMA had definite legitimate medical use. The DEA held nine days of hearings about its intention to schedule MDMA. Witnesses supporting Greer and his colleagues testified that in their opinion MDMA was an invaluable and safe psychotherapeutic drug. The DEA countered that there was no hard evidence to support this, only word of mouth.

Judge Young, who led the hearings, issued his findings on 22 May 1986. He found that MDMA did not meet any criteria necessary for scheduling. In his opinion:

- MDMA had a safe professional medical use;
- MDMA had no great potential for abuse;
- MDMA should be placed not in Schedule I but Schedule III, which allows medics to use and prescribe a drug but not for the public to buy it over the counter.

LAWN BLOWER

The Reagan-appointed DEA administrator John Lawn refused to accept the judge's recommendation. He announced that, from 13 November 1986, MDMA would be permanently placed in Schedule I.

Unsurprisingly, the medical community - in this instance fronted by Harvard professor Lester Grinspoon - retaliated with a lawsuit against the DEA. Surprisingly, it was successful and the federal court temporarily removed MDMA's Schedule I status pending reconsideration by the DEA. The DEA duly reconsidered - and duly threw MDMA back into Schedule I. They cited these reasons:

- Unapproved so-called therapeutic use of MDMA continued in many sections of the USA;
- An escalation of clandestine MDMA production, distribution and abuse was occurring nationwide;
- There was an open promotion of MDMA as a legal street drug in some areas;
- An estimated 30,000 dosage units of MDMA were distributed each month in one Texas city;
- Drug-abuse ventures reported MDMA-related incidents among patients (MDMA had neurotoxic effects on rats and monkeys - see Chapter 4).

GLEE PUBLICITY

The lawsuit had one unintended consequence: it gave MDMA the sort of free mass publicity for which advertising agents would willingly sell their grandmothers.

Suddenly an awful lot of people learned about a substance called MDMA that encouraged empathy and inhibited hostility. US MDMA use increased from a reported 10,000 instances during the whole of 1976 to 30,000 doses in a single month in 1985. The DEA went further - it reported that it was those sturdy Texans alone who were taking these 30,000 monthly doses. A 1987 survey showed that 40 per cent of students at Stanford University in California had used MDMA.

Gradually the younger and wilder new users - those outside the USA as well as within it - realised that this might be the exact substance to enhance their particular hobby: wearing kids' clothes and dancing in warehouses. All it needed was a snappier name...

DISCORD OF THE DANCE

MDMA was never intended as a recreational drug, let alone a 'dance' one. It was not particularly devised with any purpose in mind, but eventually found its ideal use as a psychotherapeutic drug under the guidance of Alexander Shulgin. As such, it would today carry no greater stigma than prescription drugs like Valium or Prozac.

The fact that young people diverted MDMA into a dance drug was of invaluable benefit to the stagnating club scenes of Europe and the US, but an accordingly massive loss to the world of psychotherapy. Even if MDMA was to be legalized as a therapeutic prescription drug, it could never be exploited for commercial purposes because of its 1914 patent. Before marketing MDMA, a drug company would need to hold exclusive rights to sell the drug, in order to recoup the expensive costs of the trials that would necessarily take place. Ecstasy looks likely to remain a dance drug indefinitely.

Shulgin, as I wrote, did not really bother himself over the physical effects of MDMA so long as the mental ones were sufficiently beneficial. To discover both the mental and physical effects of taking MDMA – and therefore who was right in the therapists vs DEA litigation described earlier – we will need to look in depth at the health qualities of ecstasy.

04 HEALTH

'That drug can kill just as easily as a bullet between the eyes if proper medical treatment is not rendered immediately.'

- Chicago Police Department officer in an e-mail to the author

'If ANYONE comes up to my children with a dangerous illegal drug I WILL SHOOT HIM DEAD... I'm not against aspirin, I'm against chemicals that destroy people's brains and lives.'

- 33-year-old technical writer from Salem, New Hampshire, in an e-mail to the author

'While I am convinced this drug is very safe in the hands of knowledgeable users, some of the patterns of use among young people are of very real concern. The message of "this drug will fry your brain if you use it, period" has led many people, upon realizing that most users don't have any problems, to assume that the warnings have no credibility at all, leading to some excessive use that probably can, in fact, produce damage to the serotonin nerves. (Some users report taking over a dozen pills in a night.)

'On another risk, MDMA doesn't appear to damage the liver normally, but can become toxic if the user becomes hyperthermic (presumably, the higher temperature inactivates critical enzymes or leads to energy exhaustion, leaving the liver unable to cope with the MDMA.) Several users have died from liver damage, with a handful more surviving only because of liver transplants.'

- 'Little John', a US biochemist, in an e-mail to the author

NOT GUILT-E

Ecstasy does not kill. The most upsetting aspect of seeing snaps of teenagers' corpses alongside those of their earlier smiling selves in tabloid newspapers is its counterproductivity. It's very useful for voyeurs, but not at all helpful for reasoned debate. (Don't believe me about voyeurs? I refer you to my research for this book, when I typed the name of heroin fatality 'Rachel Whitear' into the Google search engine: the most frequently visited page on the subject carried pictures of her corpse with the heading 'For educational purposes only – no wanking'.) The parents of Leah Betts and Lorna Spinks in the UK were indeed courageous to allow their dead or dying children's images to be displayed for the ostensible greater good. They were also misguided; ecstasy does not kill.

For sure, things associated with ecstasy can and occasionally do kill, but the constituent drug MDMA decidedly does not. When you have a love dove in your sweaty mitt, it's a case of both 'Who you are' and 'It's not what you've got, it's what you do with it'. Leah Betts died of water intoxication having taken a single unadulterated ecstasy tablet. Her best friend took the exact same brand and dosage, and lived to rave again.

DIFFERENT STROKES

Ecstasy affects people differently. This is true both physically and psychologically. You cannot overdose on MDMA, but you can, and will, respond differently from other people to its effects. People who have died because of taking ecstasy were the wrong people to take it or (to reverse the cliché) in the wrong place at the wrong time. Either that or what they took wasn't just MDMA. As I've now re-reiterated, Pure MDMA does not kill. Here is what it does do.

CHEMICAL EFFECTS OF MDMA ON THE THOUGHT PROCESSES

This is hard for non-scientists like me to grasp. It requires looking beyond the brain as just some grey spongy thing inside your skull into a convoluted organ made up of billions of individual cells. These are called neurons, and it's with these that the thought process (in as much as it's yet been measured) starts.

WOODY HEADPACKER

The 1972 Woody Allen film *Everything You Always Wanted To Know About Sex But Were Afraid To Ask* depicts the human body as controlled by tiny men and woman operating machines. This of course invites the reductio ad absurdum question of whether said tiny men and women have proportionately tinier men and women operating *their* own bodies. In Allen's vision, the brain is a control room overseen by Burt Reynolds. If only it was as simple as that.

THAT'S WHAT YOU THINK

With invaluable help from my American friend 'Little John', a professional biochemist who for obvious reasons uses a pseudonym, here is an idiot's guide to MDMA and the thought process.

THE BLOB

Once MDMA is ingested (as opposed to injected, smoked or snorted), it dissolves, enters the bloodstream and is carried to the brain neurons. This is where the fun starts.

In reality, the brain is not a control room but a control blob occupied by the aforementioned cells (neurons). There are 100 billion of these and, romantic souls that they are, they attempt to hold hands with each other via very long (in a microscopic, very short sort of way) tendril-like nerve fibres (axons) and shorter ones (dendrites). Unfortunately, the tendrils can't quite reach to hold hands, and consequently there is a gap (synapse) between them.

I WANNA HOLD YOUR DENDRITE

Looking at a single neuron, you'd see a 'big' blob (the main cell body) and a bunch of little branch-like projections. Typically, these projections are several axons and a bunch of dendrites. The dendrites are feelers – they reach out to other neurons, trying to pick up signals. The axons are 'patch cables', used to send signals to other neurons.

Each individual neuron generates a voltage. We are therefore talking electricity here. If charged atoms (ions) enter the neuron, there is an electrical signal lasting 0.01–0.02 seconds. Anyone of the 100 billion neurons will attempt to send the signal up the tendrils to its immediate neighbour neurons.

CHASMIC CHEMICALS

Axons, as I said, can be extremely long, reaching deep into remote parts of the brain, while dendrites are usually fairly short. The axon from one neuron and the dendrites from others lie quite close to each other, leaving the synapse between them.

It's a bit of a nuisance, that synapse. The signal has to resort to chemicals, and is sent across the gap by chemicals called neurotransmitters. It is as if the signal drives in a car to the synapse, boards a boat (the neurotransmitter in this analogy) to cross the synapse, docks in at the next dendrite along, then takes another car to the following neuron, where it sets off another electrical signal, and so on.

EMOTIONAL MOMENT

The two relevant neurotransmitters to MDMA are called serotonin and dopamine. There are a number of separate regulatory nerve networks in the brain that do different things. In order to prevent one from interfering with another, they use different neurotransmitters to send their own signals. The system that uses serotonin heavily influences emotional state (depression, love and so on), while dopamine controls alertness, arousal and energy levels. Anti-depression drugs like Prozac or 5-hydroxytryptophan (5-htp, which is the chemical your body makes serotonin from) increase serotonin levels in the synapse to elevate mood, while amphetamines like Ritalin increase dopamine levels to produce greater focus and energy.

The ends of the axons produce and store neurotransmitters (with the serotonin neurons making and storing serotonin, the dopamine neurons making and storing dopamine, and so on). When a serotonin neuron wants to send a signal, the axon releases serotonin into the synapse. This serotonin drifts around randomly, occasionally bumping into 'receptors' on the dendrites. When the serotonin binds to a serotonin receptor on a dendrite, that neuron receives a signal (which may result in any number of additional signals). Therefore, a serotonin neuron's axon releases serotonin, whereas the dendrites of the neighbouring neurons detect it with serotonin receptors on their surface.

While the signal is traversing the synapse, we are no longer talking electricity; we are talking chemistry, and drugs such as MDMA are chemicals. It is in this synapse stage that thought becomes a chemical process and the application of external chemicals makes its impact.

NEAR SERTAINTY

Where this gets interesting is what happens next to the released serotonin. 'Housekeeping' enzymes in the synapse (monoamine oxidase being the most famous) destroy some of it. Also, some of it is pulled back into the axon that released it. The axon does this with protein 'pumps' in its cell wall called serotonin reuptake transporters (SERTs). (Prozac increases serotonin levels in the synapse by blocking these SERTs. Although I'm focusing on serotonin, the other neurotransmitter systems work in the same way.)

So, in the normal drug-free system the axon releases serotonin into the synapse, the nearby dendrites detect it with receptors, the serotonin is then partially destroyed by enzymes in the synapse and partially recycled by getting sucked back into the axon by the SERTs.

PARTY POOPER

MDMA will have none of that technobabble. It doesn't understand a word of it. When ecstasy enters the brain, it does its own sweet thing. First, a molecule of MDMA attaches to a SERT. Blocking the SERTs alone would affect serotonin levels, as the axon would be unable to remove it from the synapse.

MDMA goes further, much further – the SERT pulls it into the axon. Once inside, it wedges the SERT open, allowing a serotonin molecule to be transported back out, exchanging serotonin for MDMA in the synapse. This effect of MDMA essentially forces the SERTs to run in reverse, moving serotonin from the axon into the synapse (where it would normally work just the opposite way), resulting in very high levels of serotonin in the synapse.

As the serotonin levels increase, the receptors on the nearby dendrites are being triggered more and more often, leading to high levels of activity within the serotonin nerve network, causing the cognitive disruptions and feelings of empathy and security typical of the MDMA experience.

To put in another way, a lot of impostor neurotransmitters are gatecrashing the neuron love-in.

THE MINUSCULE PRETENDERS

These impostor neurotransmitters (in far higher doses) desensitize receptive neurons, slow the next electrical signal and distort communications between other brain regions.

While serotonin is the primary system impacted, dopamine levels are also increased. This happens in part because the MDMA molecule fits into the dopamine reuptake transporters (making it harder for the dopamine neurons to remove dopamine from their synapses) and in part because high levels of serotonin trigger the release of additional dopamine. These elevated levels of synaptic dopamine provide the speedy feeling of almost limitless energy, and potential anxiety.

SEROTONIN BLUES

As I mentioned above, there are enzymes in the synapse that break down chemicals like dopamine and serotonin quite effectively. By placing a large amount of the brain's serotonin supply in the synapse for hours on end, much of the brain's serotonin is destroyed. How much depends on dose. MDMA users 'come down' in part because the amount of the drug in their system has gone down, but also in large part because they're running low on serotonin. It is the excess serotonin that really creates the high. The resulting lower serotonin levels are what lead to anxiety and depression after use in some individuals. If a very high dose is used, the brain's supply of serotonin can be effectively completely destroyed. Since serotonin production is a slow process, it can take weeks to recover even if no damage is done. Likewise, frequent use of MDMA can also drive down your serotonin reserves one step at a time. Since running low on serotonin messes around with concentration, memory, emotional stability, and even sleep, this is in itself a bad thing, but it has another potential risk.

NEUROTOXIC WASTERS

Remember that the MDMA molecule primarily acted on the SERTs, but also had some affinity for the dopamine reuptake transporters? The similarity between these two transporters has another consequence: the serotonin neurons can take up dopamine as well as serotonin. This doesn't normally happen to much extent, because the SERTs have a much higher affinity for serotonin – if there's plenty of serotonin around, not much dopamine should get in. However, when serotonin levels in the synapse have collapsed, dopamine comes in. This is a problem because, once inside, enzymes break down the dopamine.

RADICAL MEASURES

These breakdown products (metabolites) of dopamine include free radicals: highly destructive chemicals that can oxidize almost anything around them. It's important to note that MDMA neurotoxicity doesn't actually kill brain cells – it damages or destroys the axons they need to send signals to other neurons. (You've seen oxidation at work when slices of apple turn brown.)

There's some very good evidence to think that this is the mechanism of neurotoxicity:

- If you give rats a drug that destroys their dopamine system and then give them MDMA at doses that should cause neurotoxicity, no neurotoxicity occurs;
- If you give rats neurotoxic doses of MDMA and then give them Prozac up to six hours later, they suffer little damage (or none at all);
- Giving rats large doses of antioxidants (free-radical scavengers) like vitamin C also prevents damage (supporting the theory that damage results from oxidative stress);
- Giving the rats on (normally) neurotoxic doses of MDMA 5-htp also reduces or prevents damage.

Having gone through all that new information, we discover that perhaps there's a little more to it. You see, the serotonin neurons are normally capable of withstanding quite a bit of oxidative stress.

A sign advertising ecstasy purity-testing equipment, at the Glastonbury Music Festival, 26 June 1999.

Howard Marks (RIGHT) looks on as ecstasy is tested at a squat party in 1998.

Ecstasy testing at Green Party, Old Street, London, 1998.

CREAM-CRACKERED

Why couldn't they save themselves after a huge dose of MDMA? The answer, we think, is that they just plain ran out of energy. The SERTs (which have working like mad during the high) don't work for free – they are indirectly powered by glucose (the sugar your body uses as temporary energy storage). A long, hard MDMA high uses up a lot of this glucose, leaving the neurons unable to prevent and repair damage quickly when the dopamine starts to get in.

So, MDMA depletes serotonin and energy reserves, letting dopamine get into the serotonin neurons and leaving them too weak to defend themselves against the damage. (Important note: While the body creates glucose for temporary energy storage, any of the common sugars can be used to provide energy to the cells. You don't see many fizzy drinks with glucose in them, but sucrose will work just as well for replenishing energy.)

Energy depletion is very closely linked to hyperthermia, making avoiding overheating even more important (see p121).

PROZAC PROACTIVITY

MDMA neurotoxicity doesn't just happen; it happens under a very specific set of circumstances and can be prevented. The risk factors are doses either large enough or frequent enough to critically exhaust serotonin levels, particularly when combined with exhaustion of energy reserves. The most effective way to prevent damage seems to be simply to deny dopamine access to the serotonin neurons. This is best accomplished by supporting serotonin levels by keeping use moderate and infrequent, and by taking 5-htp.

Drugs that also block access to the serotonin neurons (like Prozac) also work, but can have complications of their own. Making sure that you get plenty of calories during and after the roll might also prevent damage – keep a good supply of sugar (juice, fizzy drinks, 'sports drinks' and so on).

HEALTH-E FREAKS

Internet E users take their personal welfare very seriously. A cursory glance at bulletin boards will reveal all manner of self-appointed, dubiously qualified 'experts' in the field. Here's a typical example (the answers are by a self-appointee, Bob Wallace, who signs his own posts with 'just my opinion' – so don't look upon him as the definitive voice of medical expertise):

Q: Do I need to bother with the four methods for preventing neurotoxicity [[taking 5-htp, prozac, a monoamine oxidase inhibitor (MAOI) or a dopamine synthesis inhibitor] if I keep to fewer than three tablets per session?

A: Nobody knows. Really. Personally, from what I've read, I think one tablet (eg around 100–120mg of MDMA) is (for a person of average weight and metabolism) below the neurotoxic threshold, at least if not repeated more than 1–2 times a month, though even at this level I would recommend the anti-neurotox methods. I also think the people taking more than three pills, every weekend, are probably into neurotoxic exposure levels, and really should use protective measures. The two-to-three-pill level, done (say) two to three times a month, is (in my mind) uncertain. None of the research seems specific enough to clarify this.

Q: Are the toxic effects proportional to the amount of MDMA taken, or do they only start to kick in when a certain dosage is exceeded in one session?

A: Damage, both in animal brains to axons and to human brains in the memory studies, does appear to be related to dose taken (and frequency of use to some extent). One interesting element is that blood level of MDMA is not linear by dose: at some dose (probably varies between people, perhaps around 3 pills) blood levels go up more rapidly. This could be due to saturating some enzyme system.

Q: If the latter, then what is this dosage?

A: This is the unknown area. In animal studies, scientists can closely control doses and do brain slices to see actual damage, but the dose scaling difficulties and differences in the brains make conclusions at these boundary dose levels hard to interpret. Human studies have all been of real people using street ecstasy and other drugs, and (even worse) compared these users with other people who may naturally have brain differences; the exceptions are one small study which tested 15 people before and after they entered the rave scene, and one study with before-and-after PET scans that showed 120mg (1.7mg/kg) did not show any measurable changes in axons (though the accuracy here was only within about one per cent).

A study to tell if somewhat higher doses produce damage in humans would have to expose MDMA-naive subjects to a reasonable chance of damage, which would make the studies not ethical and so not able to pass the required human subject review boards. The only allowable study which would produce enough data would follow, say, several hundred people from age 18 to 21, some percentage of which would do ecstasy at various dose levels, and do memory testing and brain scans every year. This would cost in the hundreds of thousands of dollars and (of course) take several years, and so has not been done.

Q: I'm curious as to what makes the axons want to take the dopamine and serotonin back in again in the first place.

A: It appears MDMA somehow alters the transporter to make it less selective; kind of like bribing the doorman at a club to let your friends in for free.

Q: So once they're aroused, they indiscriminately gobble up everything floating around loose in the synaptic cleft, right?

A: Well, dopamine as well as serotonin anyway...

Q: In which case, won't any dopamine released by taking just one or two tablets also get taken back in, causing the same type of damage (though less in proportion to the amount taken) as with a larger dose?

A: Well, probably yes, but like other toxic effects there's a level at which the axon recovers from the damage, and a higher level where there is just too much damage and the axon end dies. The damage is probably related to some kind of oxidation effect as well as the dopamine, since various anti-oxidants (as well as the reuptake transporter block by an SSRI) reduce the damage.

Q: Finally, I'd like to know what happens to the dopamine if you do manage to block it out of the axons – does it just seep harmlessly away into your bloodstream or what? If so, how long does this take? That would seem to have some bearing on how long u have to leave it before your next roll.

A: I think excess dopamine gets metabolized away by MAOB, or finds its way to a 'proper' dopamine reuptake transporter in a dopamine axon. This would happen pretty quickly, I think – minutes or a few hours.

E-NIGMA VARIATIONS

Ecstasy brings the phrase 'All things to all people' into a whole new, hot and sweaty arena of meaning. Even by narcotic standards, its effects are rarely the same twice, are rarely the same for different people and, indeed, you can't quantify it. The only evidence is the testimony of users. The vaguest and most general consensus is that:

- there are initial feelings of nausea, which soon go away;
- there is a mild euphoric rush, at about 20 to 40 minutes;
- the rush rescinds and is followed by feelings of serenity, calmness and dissipation of hostility and anger;
- those pioneers who admit to taking the drug anally (those who boldly insert E where no E has gone before) report a smoother 'coming up' and a 30 per cent more effective chemical release;
- a gradual comedown can involve tiredness and mood swings (this is hard for parents to detect, because teenagers behave like this anyway);
- there follows a hangover, due to lack of sleep, that lasts for three days or so – far longer than an alcohol hangover;
- MDMA is not an aphrodisiac as such, but the feelings of empathy it causes can inspire couples to have casual sex, which they may regret – even by casual-sex standards – when they awake the following morning (or more likely afternoon), as I explain below;

- MDMA can lessen the predatory sexual natures of men – cattle markets are rare in raves;
- intercourse on E is especially sensual, because of the heightened perceptions induced by the drug, but orgasms are often inhibited and men can suffer the same sexual dysfunction that beer drinkers call 'brewer's droop';
- there is a heightened perception of surroundings and audio signals, without the hallucinations associated with LSD; MDMA is therefore to some extent a 'mind-expanding' drug (there are indications that a small part of the MDMA can be converted into the more hallucinogenic parent drug MDA in the body, which might cause hallucinations with large doses).

TESTIMONIES

To illustrate this true multiplicity of effects, here are some varying testimonies from correspondents. The first two recount the first experiences of young people with the ecstasy roll – the first at a rave venue, the second in a married couples' house.

RAVE 'N' ROLL

'My Pauline conversion came about at a friend's birthday. As a recent convert to rave, he was insistent that we give it a proper go, and that meant taking E, which he graciously supplied (at knock-down prices). We went to Club UK in south London; a club that had a good rep in those days (since closed down for drugs problems, including a death outside the venue). To say my friends and I saw the light is an understatement. The joy of coming up on an E, surrounded by your mates in a packed, friendly club with the right music pumping through your brain is incomparable. That moment ranks among the best in my life, and you then spend years trying to chase that first experience (coming close many times I have to say). I was also lucky enough to "come up" while "Access All Areas" (a rave classic) was playing, and for that reason I am tempted to be cremated to the song (although Prodigy's "Firestarter" has to be nominated for amusement value alone).'

HOME COMFORTS

31 DECEMBER 1998, 19:30

'I went round to my neighbour's house clutching four cans of lager, only to be told they were going out. After a couple of minutes quiet talking, they said I could come with them.

'This married couple were "G" and "J". Even though they are over ten years older than me, they are still my best friends. Before they moved on to the estate, I had only smoked tobacco and had an occasional drink. They let me try a bit of cannabis; I found it to be much more relaxing and quite often couldn't stop myself from laughing!

'Before we left I drank two cans and had a joint, but I felt sober and straight.'

20:30

'A five-minute drive up the road took us to a small house belonging to "M" and "S", whom which I also knew, but not very well. Everybody was chatting and rolling joints, including myself, but I was the only one drinking. The (cheap) alcohol didn't really do much for me, I didn't seem to be getting stoned much either.'

23.00

'"G" asked how I was feeling. I said that I didn't feel even a tiny bit drunk. He replied "Never mind". So I watched the New Year celebrations on TV for while, feeling quite disappointed with the evening.'

23.40

'I notice everyone looking at me, quietly whispering to each other (it wasn't paranoia!). "J" was signalling with her finger that she wanted me to walk over.

'I see pills on the table, they had a bird like symbol on them, and I knew instantly that these were not "normal" tablets. There was one that had been cut in half, "J" pointed to it, and I was given a bit of lecture, not being told off, but being prepared for a new experience.

'"Sip a pint of water every hour."

'"When you start feeling something, tell us."

'Feeling a little bit worried, I drank my water rather quickly, and was told not to panic. The music: *A Retrospective Of House 1991-1995*. Very happy house music.

'I can't remember the night in great detail, but here is a bit of what I can remember.'

1 JANUARY 1999, 00:20

'I start to smile. I asked if anyone had turned the music up. No one had. The room became slightly "brighter". I didn't need to say anything, everyone else just smiled back. I said, "I feel amazing!"'

00:40

'The amazing feeling progressed to an even more amazing feeling; I closed my eyes and just listened to the music. It made my whole body tingle. I opened my eyes and "J" walked over to me. She ran her fingernails through my hair. WOW! The rush was very intense, but not at all unpleasant. My head and hair kept tingling, for about 30 seconds afterwards, amazing!'

03:00

'Heavier music was put on. "G" said "See you later! You will just drift away." I just melted into my chair...'

06:00

'Time to go home. I was quite astounded to see "G" driving, not something that I would advise, but he is without doubt the best driver I know. I arrive home and go to bed.'

08:30

'I wake up feeling surprisingly refreshed. I sort myself out ready for work. (Yes, work! I forgot to mention it to the others!) I had to do a four-hour shift on New Year's Day. I can honestly say it was the quickest four hours of my life!'

14:30
'On my way home I visit my neighbours just to recollect the previous night's events. At some point during the night I had taken another half, but I couldn't remember it!

'Apparently I told them that I love them all, and they meant a lot to me. Powerful stuff!'

PRACTICE MAKES PERFECT

Like sex, pill popping improves with practice. However, due to the variety of pills resulting from global trafficking, there are always surprises to be had – not to mention damp squibs.

A contact, and a decided dab hand in the ecstasy scene, wrote me of a new E brand that singularly failed to wash whiter: 'I am a regular raver, and i have never been to a rave sober. just a couple days ago, my friend offered me some pills. He hooked me up with them, no doubt, but i didnt know how what effect they would have on me. They were called triple stack white dome. That doesnt really matter, but I took one on wednesday (it is saturday now). I took a quarter of it; didnt do much for me. 15 minutes later I took another quarter, and then the rest of the pill (a half), 30 minutes later. I had forgot how long it takes ecstasy to kick in. That was a really nice roll, but it wasnt quite what i was expecting. It lasted about two hours. The next day i took a half first. Then when it kicked in, I took another half, so that when I hit my peak it would hit me. I was rollin quite well, although not as good as the day before. I then took the other pill about an hour from when I took the second half. This provided somewhat (not much) of a rise in intoxication. When the day was over, I recorded the times I took the pills and how long it lasted. It wasnt as long as the first day, I wonder why? On Friday, I decided to take a whole pill. I didn't know if I could handle it, but then I realized I had taken much

'I don't think that there is such a thing as a safe level, a safe dose of ecstasy, and we have yet to be able to evaluate the long term health effects so I think it would be wholly wrong to downgrade ecstasy from class A to class B.' Bob Ainsworth, Home Office minister with responsibility for drugs policy in the UK

more severe doses in the past (i had taken 'shrooms with E, K and E, and Acid, although the acid only gave me a slight body high and a headache). I took the pill, and about 40 min later it hit me (the usual time it takes for the X to kick in). it wasnt as hard as wednesday, but harder than thursday. It was a more peaceful roll, but i fell asleep about an hour and a half after it kicked in! I was laying down (listening to VERY LOUD trance), when I just fell asleep. can someone tell me why these things happened? the X hits me much harder and much better at a rave than at home. Maybe it could be the enviroment? Maybe. Maybe Not. E is a pretty social drug, but taking it alone can be fun too. My only experience taking it alone was bad but I took two VERY strong pills and I suspect there was some meth in them too. Everyone else was taking half pills from this same batch and I didn't find out until too late. I think one pill taken alone is fairly safe.'

OLD HEAVE HO

Ecstasy isn't just the in drug for the young 'uns. This testimony comes from a respectable 50 year old: 'The drug removes all your neuroses. It takes away the fear of response. There is an overwhelming sense of peace, you are at peace with the world. You feel open, clear, tender. I can't imagine that anyone is angry under its influence, or selfish or mean or defensive. You have lots of insight into yourself, real insight, which you hold on to after the experience is gone.'

E-CREATE

Last of the positive testimonies comprises another Internet question-and-answer session, addressing that overriding concern of the arty-farty bohemian-esque druggie: will MDMA squeeze the creative juices whilst discarding the bitter pith?

Q: I will not be doing any dancing or raving. I plan on getting into some watercolour painting, or I might blitz my flat (well that is the plan anyway) I have taken loads of speed in the past, and was hoping to use E the same way. Can you get into things like this on Es?

A: Yes. You may find you are more creative on E. People use low doses for writing and stuff.

Q: Or am I going to start to want to go out and be with people, or feel freaked out?

A: I've gotten paranoia on E but I'm that way by nature anyway. 90 percent of people or more are very social on E. It's like coke in that respect but I think E feels more natural.

Q: Also, there is this matter of water and dehydration. Will I need to drink loads of water if I am not dancing?

A: Be careful. You aren't likely to get dehydrated while painting of course so go easy on the water. Drink a moderate amount. People have died from drinking too much water on E, it causes low sodium levels.

Q: Is it advisable to drink alcohol or not, or smoke pot?

A: Only drink a little while on E, I like E alone mostly. I get a pretty big buzz with pot on E, but again I vastly prefer doing E alone. I think most things ruin E. I think it might mix well with acid or maybe some downer on the comedown but that's all. Maybe a couple of beers while it's fading.

Q: Tell me also how long do the effects last?

A: Don't eat too much before the pill. One time my onset was delayed by three hours because of that. Normally it hits you at T-plus 45 to 60 minutes. Peak at T-plus 120 I think. Plateau for a bit and maybe done at about T-plus four hours. I've had after-effects up to 12 or more hours later but I had done six rolls over the course of a night.

Q: How long does it take to affect you after ingestion? Is there any comedown at all, like with speed?

A: For me, yes. Sometimes it's unpleasant and most of my friends then begin a search for more E to come back up again. I find it addictive but only over the course of a night and it's more psychological than anything. Looking back, I think it's better to err on the side of too little E than too much E.

Roll in moderation seems to be the advice of that Netted sage. It's usually the best advice in any context. Maximizing the ecstasy effect requires a combination of dedication to the cause, and the benefit of experience from those who have trodden that euphoric road before.

BANANA E-PUBLIC

Another raving wise man recommends consuming the fruits of herbaceous tropical trees as a healthy ecstatic dessert course: 'Bananas provide sugar. That's a good thing while you're rolling... Your body is using up sugar at a rapid rate. They also contain minerals like potassium (important for the nervous system, among other things) and also contain dopamine precursors (which can help the high).'

DOWNERS

Bad ecstasy experiences are usually due to higher doses. Like LSD, the experience (for good or ill) depends on the mood of the user, the expectations of the user and the amenability of the surroundings. Bad experiences include the following:

- visual and auditory hallucinations;
- anxiety attacks;
- confusion;
- panic;
- insomnia;
- psychosis;
- LSD-type flashbacks if the drug is used continually;
- traumatic events or negative emotions brought to the surface of those who have tried to use the drug as a self-psychotherapeutic drug without professional guidance.

An E guru provides this sound advice: 'It takes anywhere from one to two weeks for your serotonin to rebuild. Doing ecstasy many days in a row, or a lot of pills in a night, doesn't really get you "higher" on MDMA. Once your serotonin is depleted, you're not getting high off of the MDMA in the pill anymore, you're just getting high off of the fillers (crystal, caffeine, ketamin, whatever is in it), and as your sleep deprivation gets greater and greater you will feel higher but it's only because of the sleep deprivation.'

Again, there are multitudes of testimonies to back this up. This one comes from a druggie of a previous generation checking out this newfangled ecstasy lark: 'Well after dropping my first E, I can say I don't think I will be doing it again. I dropped half a tab and waited for an hour before dropping the rest. Within half an hour of dropping the second half I thought to myself I hope this don't get anymore intense, it was on the whole an uncomfortable experience (very chemical I thought, and some sweating also. The tabs had been chemically tested I learnt and did contain MDMA), it was changeable though, and there were pleasant times but I was glad when it all ended. I have not taken stimulants for over eight years so that might have something to do with it. It was not like speed or acid, but it did feel a lot like 'shrooms I thought, but without the hallucinations. I did some yoga and that was good, the way in which my body moved and flowed with ease and without pain or discomfort, and music sounded brilliant. I couldn't sleep for over 36 hours after taking it, and felt slightly disoriented the next day and also had a headache. I took some codeine to chill out later the next day and it wasn't until after I eventually slept did I feel normal again. It was an interesting experience, but I doubt if I will repeat it. It is definitely a young people and party drug. I could imagine if I was out in the countryside with nature and a group of people around a campfire, the experience would have been more rewarding. Being an "old fart" I suppose my metabolism can't handle it the way it used to, or I have been spoilt by all the years of good pharmaceuticals

In the UK according to official reports, there are 430,000 users, who spend a total of £300 million ($435 million) a year on ecstasy, perhaps taking between one and five pills a night. Unofficial surveys state it could be twice this figure.

and other drugs now obsolete, that resulted from pharmacy break ins and other sources in the '60s and '70s. I will stick with the opiates I think.'

STARK RAVING MAD

An anonymous correspondent to the UK *Guardian* newspaper of 1 January 2002 wrote this missive of New Year's cheer: 'After taking [ecstasy], our son experienced a deep depression and progressed to becoming very psychotic, inhabiting in his mind a terrifying world unrelated to reality. He was admitted as an emergency to a psychiatric ward. There were periods of lucidity and, with lots of love, he recovered. It took six months. He suffered a lot and so did we. The MDMA content of ecstasy tablets can vary by 70-fold and they can contain a variety of other substances - you haven't a clue what you're getting. In addition ecstasy (and, I understand, cannabis) can trigger longer-term mental problems in some susceptible people. Yes, the casualty departments on New Year's Eve will no doubt be full of alcohol-related cases. Sadly, I'm sure the psychiatric wards will also be coping with people with drug-induced psychosis - who had no idea that ecstasy could have these effects.'

'Susceptible people' is, of course, the key phrase here. The drug consumed by the son had seemingly triggered a latent psychiatric disorder. The correspondent is indeed right that ecstasy and cannabis can trigger such effects - but then so can alcohol, chocolate and spaghetti bolognaise made with too much garlic. It isn't the drug itself, but the person who takes it, who's at fault in these instances.

OD-EAR

The Internet gurus do not always couch their responses in the PLUR idiom. In response to an earnest inquiry from an ecstasy newcomer (this is the rave dialect, as explained on p10, at its broadest) - 'i red sum were that u can od on 1600 mg of pure mdma thats about 12-16 caps (pills, tabs, wat ever u cal it) thats a hell of a lot and i think thats all at once' - an expert in the field who seems to take his approach from the TV doctor *Becker*, though curiously names himself after ex Ethiopian emperor and benefactor Haile Selassie, proffered this blunt advice: 'you cant vomit chemicals already absorbed and into the bloodstream and metabolized by the body you stupid fucking kid... grow the fuck up you piece of teenage ghetto trash... i suppose you also believe in the tooth fairy, santa claus the easter bunny and the boogey man you gullible piece of urban legend-believing trash vermin... read a book or two and educate yourself you brainless, single digit IQ bastard result of your slutty mom screwing the trashman.' Nice bloke.

A FUNGI TO BE WITH

E does not only extract its narcotic toll. There is also a physical toll to pay in a currency that includes scabs, rashes, fungi and body odour.

Professional typists complain of repetitive strain injury; joggers, themselves on a high from the body's very own amphetamine endorphins, can take on more exercise than their bodies can cope with and end up injuring themselves. Typists, though, only move their fingers; joggers only exercise for maybe an hour. Ravers are more committed than that; they can move their entire bodies intensely and vigorously for the *whole night*. No wonder they collect unsavoury skin conditions like trainspotters collect numbers. Blemishes to be found on many ravers' persons include these beauties:

- damaged joints and backs due to dancing on a concrete floor;
- fungal and viral infections of the foot;
- unsightly and itchy yeast infections in the groin area;
- friction burns on the arse cheeks, known as 'raver's rash';
- damaged foot joints, known as 'techno toe';
- chunks of flesh gouged out due to tightening and convulsions of the jaw (those babies' dummies are not only a fashion accessory; they are a very practical gumshield).

EVERYTHING YOU DIDN'T WANT TO KNOW ABOUT SEX AND WERE AGHAST TO ASK

Casual unprotected sex carries the usual moist cachet of possible pregnancy, sexually transmitted diseases and feelings of guilt/disgust when you wake up in the juices of someone you would not usually touch with the proverbial ten-foot barge shunter.

In its favour, though, E is likely to inspire mutual, considerate intercourse. Considering the list of unpleasant complaints listed above, that is probably just as well. The thought of making breakfast for someone with whom you have just spent a night exchanging bodily fluids and groinal yeast infections should be sufficient to deter even the randiest raver from rogering.

THAT'S JUST TAKING THE PISS

Actress Sarah Miles, of *Ryan's Daughter* fame, has admitted to drinking urine (her own, thankfully) to keep her skin clear and body healthy. It is no new practice - indeed canny Medieval quacks used to piss in a bottle and sell it as a mouthwash - but there is no evidence whatsoever to back up pee's purported panacean propensities.

Ravers, however, have a very good reason to consume their own piss: 60 per cent of MDMA enters the urine unchanged. MDMA is therefore recyclable. Drink two number ones and you effectively have another ecstasy tablet free.

As far as I know, the rave generation has yet to take advantage of this cash-cutting exercise. I suggest they suck it and see.

DROP-DEAD GORGEOUS

To date, there have been around 90 E-related fatalities in the UK and around 40 in the United States. The US has far fewer fatalities because of its typically more spacious venues and lesser booze culture (see Chapter 1). Statistics of fatalities relate to the number of times MDMA is used, which is unknowable (the oft-quoted figure of a million users each weekend could be wildly exaggerated, according to private questionnaires), and the number of times someone dies afterwards, which is of uncertain meaning. On top of this confusion, regular users must increase the dose to maintain the same effect, which leaves us with the old cliché 'Which came first, the chicken or the Marengo sauce?'

However, ecstasy-related fatalities almost certainly represent a tiny minority of ecstasy consumed. One estimate, by the Council Biostatics Unit (CBU), using 1996 figures to attempt to calculate the death rate in

15–24s, came up with a rate of between one in 100,000 and one in 200,000. This makes taking ecstasy technically safer than both rugby and horse riding.

The varying effects of ecstasy on different people, coupled with a seeming non-correlation between toxicity and blood levels, makes the likelihood of fatalities very hard to estimate. Some users with high levels of MDMA in their blood survive, while a normal 100–150mg dose causes death in others. In the UK, deaths have involved a range of doses from one to five tablets in a single session.

To re-re-reiterate – ecstasy does not kill; associated causes do. There are three main causes of death.

HEATSTROKE

- MDMA speeds up the heart and blocks signals to the brain that tell the body to slow down.
- The body temperature rises above its danger limit of 40°C (104°F).
- Convulsions, dilated pupils, very low blood pressure and accelerated heart rate follow.
- Blood coagulates where it shouldn't (like the lungs) and air can't get through.
- There follows paralysis or coma and sometimes death.
- Alternatively, blood doesn't coagulate where it should, resulting in haemorrhaging from internal legions.
- Symptoms of heatstroke include grossly inflated cardiac rhythm, hyperthermia, convulsions, acute renal failure, widespread coagulation of the blood and the rupturing of tiny vessels.

WATER TOXICITY

For most ills, drinking a lot of fluid is the exact thing to do. Under MDMA, however, it can have fatal consequences. Young women are most at risk of this because of their hormonal balance.

- High levels of oestrogen can prevent their bodies from coping with water retention. On top of this the MDMA is broken down and stimulates the release of vasopressin, a hormone that encourages water retention and prevents urination.

- The break-up of MDMA also releases a chemical called HMMA that causes the woman to drink fluids.
- The concentration of sodium in the bloodstream falls dangerously low (young women require much more sodium in their bloodstream than post-menopausal women or men).
- Water is retained in sponge-like brain neurons, and the pressure shuts down primary bodily functions like breathing and heart rate.
- There follows dizziness, disorientation and possible collapse and death.
- It is far better to sip a pint of water every hour than down several pints at once. It is also wise to eat to replace sodium lost while sweating.

HEART FAILURE

- MDMA causes a significant rise in blood pressure and heart rate.
- People with formerly undiagnosed heart conditions can suddenly get an ad hoc practical diagnosis at an inconvenient moment.

GIRLFRIEND PROBLEMS

An Internet bulletin board recently carried this plea for help from a concerned raver, on behalf of his post-ecstatic girlfriend (again, this is pretty raw rave dialect): 'This was the 6th time ever over a 1 yr period she has done x. she took 2 pink genies friday nite and 1 and a half Saturday nite. she barley even rolled saturday. sunday was a normal after x day i guess. monday she started to have dizzy spells come and go every other minute. loss of appitite due to vomitting after every meal. she says she fells like shes on a drug still and its really scaring her. having trouble sleeping and worrying bad. if anyone has heard of this from x let me know how long it lasts or what i should do.

'If I felt my officers were going into nightclubs looking for people who were in possession of ecstasy then I would say to them, and I would say publicly, that they are wasting police resources... There are far more important things, which cause real harm to the community.'

Commander Brian Paddick, suspended head of Lambeth Police

oh its now tuesday night and still no change. im making her go to the dr tomorrow if she likes it or not. thanks for any advise people.'

As usual, the ever-helpful rave community could decipher the message and offer the man some practical advice: 'Yeah take her to the doctor. If she wasn't rolling, I'm thinking the pill has no MDMA in it. It most probably had a mix of more dangerous chemicals which are causing the problems. Best to take her to a doctor who can find out what that was and thus fix her up.'

GET YOUR ACT TOGETHER

An encouraging sign for the future is that proprietors of UK nightclubs (where the vast majority of E-related collapses happen) are being told in no uncertain terms to clean up their act. At the announcement of a March 2002 campaign called 'Safer Clubbing', Home Office Drugs Minister Bob Ainsworth said:

> *Although drug use has stabilized nationally, unfortunately for many young club-goers illegal drug use has become an integral part of their night out. Of particular concern are those clubbers who use a cocktail of drugs and alcohol that is likely to greatly increase the risks to their health and safety.*
>
> *Club owners and dance promoters have a duty to make sure that they have done everything possible to reduce the risks faced by the young people who are their paying customers. The Safer Clubbing guide will help them, and those that license them, to adopt best health and safety practice.*
>
> *It is important that we begin to change the culture and attitudes to drug taking that have become a lifestyle choice for so many young people enjoying the club scene. But, we have to recognize that some clubbers will continue to ignore the risks and carry on taking dangerous drugs. If we cannot stop them from taking drugs then we must be prepared to take steps to reduce the harm that they may cause themselves.*

This is encouraging because it suggests the UK Home Office is adopting a more realistic approach to drugs than its former 'Just say no' one. It issued these guidelines to help club owners comply with licensing laws:

- provide adequate supplies of drinking water;
- prevent overcrowding;
- ensure proper air conditioning and ventilation;
- take steps to prevent overheating; and
- ensure the venues comply with health and safety legislation.

Specific recommendations were:

- for clubs to hire police-approved staff to prevent the hire of criminals as door supervisors;
- that door supervisors should be trained to carry out searches;
- that security should regularly patrol all areas of the venue,
- that club staff should be trained in first aid so they can recognize and assist people who are intoxicated through drugs, alcohol or a mix of both;
- that club owners should provide a chillout room, with a calm, cool atmosphere.

Encouragingly, most commentators – including spokesmen for the police and the parents of Lorna Spinks (see Chapter 5) – have been supportive of the measures. Deputy Assistant Commissioner Michael Fuller, head of the Metropolitan Police's Drugs Directorate, said:

> *We are delighted to have contributed to the Safer Clubbing guide and welcome the launch of this multi-agency initiative. Tackling drug misuse in London is one of the Metropolitan Police Service's priorities and this initiative highlights the important role club owners and event organizers can play in reducing the risk of violence and disorder in clubs across the capital.*

Dr John Ramsey, head of the toxicology unit at St George's Hospital, London, agreed:

Safer Clubbing draws together components required to minimize the harm caused by drugs. It clearly sets out the responsibilities of all participants including clubbers themselves. It recognizes the importance that environmental factors play in safeguarding the health of clubbers and minimising the toxicity of MDLA (ecstasy), and encourages all agencies and groups to work together.

Alan and Liz Spinks also concurred:

We hope that the principles and advice contained in the Safer Clubbing guide are adopted by all those involved in the clubbing environment. The recommendations in the document are practical and pragmatic. They target the safety of clubbers and we fully endorse them. They will help to reduce the likelihood of a crisis occurring, help with its early detection and improve reaction in the critical period immediately afterwards.

LONG-TERM EFFECTS

We've established that ecstasy does not kill. Nor does it have the addictive attributes of opiates or induce the craving connected with cocaine. The perfect drug, then? Not necessarily. There is another, more disturbing, question to consider. Does E do your head in in the long term? Is there likely to be a year 2042 television (or whatever the popular medium is then) documentary featuring a sample of early 21st-century ravers, who have all been reduced to dribbling idiots over the years? Happily, there is a definite answer to this one: no one knows.

One correspondent certainly thinks it's happened to her. The fact that she appears to like the idea seems, ironically, to back up her assertion: 'E abuse has left me with permanent brain "damage", but it's not all bad! I now find myself with amazing psychic abilities, I can see in the dark, I have a photographic memory, I can take as many pills as I want without getting comedowns, i don't get hangovers from alcohol any more, I don't need to eat, I can smell and taste stuff (I always had very poor sense of smell and taste [tongue] before), oh, and I'm tripping 24/7/366!!! so it's not all bad!!!!!'

Ecstasy testing at Green Party, Old Street, London, 1998.

UK Prime Minister Tony Blair holds up a 'Dennis the Menace' ecstasy pill during a visit to Dyce Academy in Aberdeen, March 1997.

A squad of hardcore ravers, each sporting a pacifier, that essential ecstasy accessory. The dummies are used to prevent the wearer from biting out chunks of flesh due to convulsions of the jaw.

The following report from ABC News agrees with her assessment, but not her opinion as to its worth:

> UNKNOWN RISKS ACROSS THE BOARD
>
> *Ecstasy, a synthetic drug manufactured mostly in Europe, is a hallucinogenic stimulant that gives its users a feeling of euphoria. The popular drug has spread beyond rave parties to college campuses and even into middle-class, professional America. Its growing pervasiveness is troublesome because the prevailing belief is that it's perfectly safe – in part because some scientists think it might have therapeutic effects. Also, it does not produce extreme behaviors as some other illegal drugs do. It just seems to make you feel good.*
>
> *'My experience has been very safe with it, and everyone around me has been safe,' says one 29-year-old professional who runs her own business and chooses not to use her name. 'I don't know anyone who's addicted to it or has problems with it.'*
>
> *But a number of users do report a depression they call 'Suicide Tuesdays.' Dozens of people are reported to have died after ecstasy raised their body temperature to extreme levels. And scientists who study how ecstasy works in the brain say there is a great deal of evidence that should make us worry.*

LADY MUCK

Like alcohol and the police force, ecstasy makes life harder for its female participants than its male ones. Beyond the aforementioned short-term problem of sodium depletion, there is also the apparent long-term possibility of limb abnormalities in babies, as is detailed by this report from the *Daily Telegraph* of 22 October 1999:

> *Heart and limb abnormalities in babies are linked for the first time to young women using the drug ecstasy during their pregnancies.*
>
> *A study funded by the Department of Health found that heart defects were up to five times higher than expected and limb*

abnormalities were 38 times higher. Overall, the congenital defect rate was 15.4 per cent, when two to three per cent was normal. That represents 'a significantly increased risk', the researchers say today.

Dr Patricia McElhatton, head of the National Teratology Information Service, which investigates birth defects and advises doctors on drugs in pregnancy, said the results were a cause for concern. She said: 'Numbers in the study were very small and it has been quite difficult to tease the information out but we think there should now be more research into this.'

The group undertook the investigation after receiving 302 inquiries between 1989 and 1998 about taking ecstasy in pregnancy. It traced 136 women, aged between 16 and 36, who had taken ecstasy alone (74) or ecstasy and other illegal drugs and/or alcohol in pregnancy. Other drugs included cocaine, amphetamines, LSD and cannabis, heroin and methadone.

A total of 78 babies were born. The rest of the pregnancies were terminated or ended in miscarriage. The miscarriage rate was not unusual but terminations at 35 per cent was higher than average.

The report in The Lancet *says 12 babies were born with abnormalities to drug-taking mothers. One baby who had no obvious abnormalities died. This baby's mother had taken ecstasy, cocaine, heroin and methadone during the pregnancy.*

Three babies had a club foot, a rate of 38 per 1,000 live births when the national rate was one per 1,000. One baby had a toe malformation and another a skull abnormality. Heart defects in babies among mothers taking ecstasy and/or other drugs were 26 per 1,000, when five to ten for every 1,000 live births was expected.

A spokesman for the Health Education Authority said that one in ten 16 to 29-year-olds said they had used ecstasy at least once. He said: 'People should be aware of the adverse effects of taking drugs. At present ecstasy has been linked only with brain injury in later life after long-term use.'

BRAIN DRAIN

'Repeated ecstasy exposure has been shown to lead to clear brain damage and that brain damage is correlated with behavioral deficits in learning and memory processes,' says Alan Leshner, the director of the National Institute on Drug Abuse, which is a part of the US National Institute of Health. 'This is not a benign, fun drug.'

Normally, your brain controls mood partly by passing the chemical serotonin – in small amounts – from one brain cell to another. But ecstasy forces lots of serotonin across the gap. Some new research suggests it leaves brain cells weakened and may cause irreversible brain loss.

'We know from primates, non-human primates, that the damage lasts for years,' says Una McCann, a neuroscientist at Johns Hopkins University. Some scientists, on the other hand, report ecstasy may have benefits in strictly limited cases.

'One group we're interested in studying are individuals with end-stage cancer who have severe depression and anxiety and physical pain which have not responded to conventional measures,' says Charles Grob, a psychiatrist at Harbor UCLA Medical Center.

If medical use is ever allowed, it is far off. For now, government agents are battling the spread, and the myths, of a pill called ecstasy, which for them, at least, is anything but.

I AM INDEED YOUR STEPPING STONE

Were the aforementioned documentary to feature Una McCann's monkeys (and monkeys do take ecstasy – though they don't have much say in the matter), we might be able to hazard the answer that 'maybe' ecstasy causes long-term effects to the brain. It's not known if it does so in humans, though, and that's what matters. Unlike cows, no one cares about the sanity of monkeys.

CASQUE OF THE RED DEATH

Red squirrel monkeys are shy, good-natured and egalitarian simians that occupy the Pacific wet lowlands of Costa Rica and Panama. They are currently in decline because their habitats are fragmented by such concerns as deforestation, tourism, agriculture, insecticide-spraying and electrocution from power lines. Times are clearly hard for the red squirrel monkeys.

It's just as well that American scientists dole out plenty of ecstasy to cheer them up. At St John's University in New York, scientists exposed red squirrel monkeys to 5mg of MDMA twice daily for four consecutive days, while a control group was administered salt water for the same duration. (These MDMA doses were much higher and more frequent than typical human ones.) The MDMA caused neurological damage that persisted six to seven years later – nerve fibres had died and damaged neurons grew back abnormally – while the salt-water monkeys were unharmed (this is a definition of 'unharmed' that involves slicing monkeys' brains in half).The MDMA monkeys had a greater serotonin depletion in some parts of the brain than in others.

Seemingly, to readdress the vivisection balance from lovable species to unlovable ones, scientists carried out similar experiments on lab rats, with similar results, once (crucially) they took the relative sizes of the animals into account

SO WHAT?

Supporters of MDMA question whether animal experiments are of relevance to humans. Perhaps worryingly for ecstasy users, the May 2000 edition of UK medical periodical *The Lancet* suggests in an article that they may indeed be. This is significant because *The Lancet* is the definitive medics' medical magazine: it is written in medical jargon, intended to be read by medics and has no political bias. It may, in other words, be right (though, see the recent *Daily Telegraph* report quoted on pp131–3). In particular, *The Lancet* points out that these MDMA apologists are ignoring the central research principle of 'inter-species dosage scaling', which allows for the differences in body size, based on body weight and surface area.

Correlations have been established between laboratory animal species and human patients undergoing treatment. For example, the toxicity of anti-cancer drugs in laboratory animals has correlated with the toxicity observed in humans when the species doses were scaled to body surface area. This is documented with reams of evidence that pro-drugs campaigners cannot – if they're doing their job thoroughly – simply dismiss as irrelevant.

HUMAN FRUITCAKES

The very limited human research that has taken place is indefinite. Recent legal measures have allowed for limited MDMA research in the UK. Accordingly, researchers made a comparative study between the effects upon humans of MDMA and alcohol (presumably, unlike with the monkeys, there was no shortage of volunteers in either category).

The test subjects were required to count backwards in sevens from a three-figure number. The MDMA subjects made twice as many mistakes as the alcohol ones. (Rumours that they were made to recite the 'pheasant plucker' rhyme as an encore are unfounded.)

Further tests at the time (1997) seemed to confirm that ecstasy may well long-term mental health consequences, as reported in the *Daily Telegraph*:

> *Fears that use of ecstasy can cause long-term brain damage leading to depression and memory loss later in life are heightened today in a new report.*
>
> *Scans of heavy users of the drug found distinct alterations in their brains, even among those who had given up several years beforehand. The imbalance they discovered related to serotonin, a chemical that helps control depression, anxiety, memory disturbance and other psychiatric disorders.*
>
> *The authors of the study conclude today that people who use ecstasy, the drug that has epitomized the '90s club scene, are 'unwittingly putting themselves at risk of developing brain injury'.*
>
> *Their message was echoed yesterday by Prof David Smith, pharmacologist at Oxford University, who said: 'It is something that a lot of us are worried about with ecstasy, but young people don't want to know about long-term brain damage.'*
>
> *The experiment was carried out on 14 people who had formerly taken the drug on average 200 times over four to five years. They*

had stopped taking it between three weeks and several years previously. Fifteen people who had never used ecstasy were also scanned. The researchers suspected that the damage might occur to parts of brain cells known as axons, which transmit signals to neighbouring cells.

The scientists, led by Una McCann of the National Institute of Mental Health in Bethesda, Maryland, injected each person with a radioactive substance that seeks out a marker chemical found in axons.

The scans, which revealed how much radioactive substance there was in each brain, showed there was a clear difference, with much less of the marker chemical in the drug-takers. The scientists have concluded that these people have fewer brain cells capable of producing serotonin. Dr George Ricaurte, one of the authors, said: 'These losses are significant and, along with our early studies in animals, suggest that nerve cells are damaged.'

The researchers, writing in the Lancet, *said there were no signs of recovery in the people who had gone for longest without taking ecstasy. The other question was how much damage was required to cause psychological effects. Professor Smith said: 'It could be that the effects are subtle, leading to depression later on in life.'*

ON THE CONTRARY

In April 2002, contrary evidence came to light suggesting that the case for long-term brain damage was far from proven and, moreover, that, for logistical reasons, politicians have allegedly covered up inherent flaws in the tests that have been carried out. Again, the report is from the *Daily Telegraph* (19 April):

> *Much of the scientific evidence showing that ecstasy damages the brain is fundamentally flawed and has been mistakenly used by politicians to warn the public of the dangers of the drug, a report said yesterday.*

The inquiry by [UK science periodical] New Scientist *found that many of the findings on ecstasy published in respected journals could not be trusted. It said it was an 'open secret' that some researchers who failed to find impairment in ecstasy users had trouble getting their findings published.*

'Our investigation suggests the experiments are so irretrievably flawed that the scientific community risks haemorrhaging credibility if it continues to let them inform public policy,' the report said.

It found there were serious flaws in brain scans which allegedly show that ecstasy destroys nerve cells involved in the production and transport of serotonin, a vital brain chemical involved in a range of functions including memory, sleep, sex, appetite and mood.

In 1998, George Ricaurte and Una McCann at Johns Hopkins University in Baltimore published a paper in The Lancet *that seemed to provide the first evidence that ecstasy use led to lasting brain damage.*

The research involved brain scans with a radioactively tagged chemical probe that latched on to the serotonin transporter proteins that ecstasy targets. The thinking was that brains damaged by ecstasy would give off less radioactive 'glow' than those where the serotonin cells were intact.

The scan pictures, which showed the brains of ecstasy users did on average glow less, were used in public information campaigns. In America they strongly influenced harsher penalties for ecstasy offences.

But two independent experts told New Scientist *there was a key flaw. They said the way brains reacted to this kind of scan varied enormously with or without ecstasy.*

Some healthy brains glowed up to 40 times brighter than others and even a number of ecstasy users' brains outshone ecstasy-free brains by factors of 10 or more. Another study by Dutch scientists led by Liesbeth Reneman and Gerard den Heeten at the Academic Medical Centre in Amsterdam was similarly flawed.

New Scientist *said it found that 'despite the poster depiction of "your brain on ecstasy" there never was – and never has been – a typical scan showing the typical brain of a long-term ecstasy user'.*

Stephen Kish, a neuro-pathologist at the Center for Addiction and Health in Toronto, said: 'There are no holes in the brains of ecstasy users. And if anyone wants a straightforward answer to whether ecstasy causes any brain damage, it's impossible to get one from these papers.'

Marc Laruelle, an expert on brain scanning at Columbia University, New York City, said: 'All the papers have very significant scientific limitations that make me uneasy.'

Similar uncertainty surrounds evidence that ecstasy impairs mental performance. In the majority of tests of mental agility, ecstasy users performed as well as non-users.

Andrew Parrott, a psychologist at the University of East London, found that ecstasy users outperformed non-users in tests requiring them to rotate complex shapes in their mind's eye.

So at present, the answer to the question 'Does ecstasy use cause long-term brain damage?' remains as definite as ever: no one knows. The same applies to the contrary question, which admittedly comes from left side, 'Is ecstasy good for you?'

EROWID WE GO

The Erowid website – a standard reference centre for not only druggies but also new agers and others who follow 'alternative' lifestyles – thinks it might be: '[A] researcher at Harbor-UCLA Medical Center says there could be an upside to ecstasy... Charles Grob, a psychiatrist, has secured first-ever FDA approval for human trials of the drug. The experiments are designed to lead to tests of ecstasy as a possible painkiller for the terminally ill and for use in psychotherapy. "Hundreds of thousands of young people have taken it," Grob said. "But we know very little about it. There's lots of talk about potential dangers, but we want to explore it extensively." Few in the scientific community are enthusiastic about MDMA's potential benefits. Many likened advocates of its therapeutic attributes to 1960s boosters of LSD. "When LSD was first discovered, that same view of therapeutic use was popular but it turned out to be completely wrong," said Dr. Stephen Stahl, an LSD expert in the UCSD School of Medicine's Psychiatry Department.

'Nevertheless, even researchers who have found harmful results in MDMA animal trials say they approve of Grob's initial study. They say much needs to be learned about what MDMA does to the human brain and heart, and that it isn't impossible the drug may have some treatment value. "We need to get rid of the drug-war mentality and see that all drugs aren't all evil," said Dr. David Nichols, a Purdue University researcher who tested MDMA on rats in the early 1980s...

'Grob said the FDA approved his testing proposal after years of turning down similar ones. In the study's first phase, he will give ecstasy to six health professionals who have previously used MDMA on their own. He'll monitor their sleep patterns, conduct brain scans and perform a variety of other medical tests. He said he hopes to dispel some of the rumors about MDMA heard on dance floors and campuses. These include whispered reports that it drains spinal fluid and acts temporarily as an aphrodisiac, only to cause longer-term impotence. The second part of Grob's trials, which has yet to win FDA approval, will seek to determine whether ecstasy eases pain in terminal cancer patients and helps them, as a therapeutic agent, cope with the knowledge that they are going to die. Grob says those applications are "way, way down the line. That's putting the cart before the horse."

'But Rick Doblin, an unabashed proponent of psychedelic drugs, said he hopes Grob's study will open the door to MDMA's use in treating people who suffer mental illnesses, are recovering from traumatic events or just struggling with a marriage. "I think MDMA has a significant place in the future of psychiatry and then in a liberalized world where adults have free choice for these kinds of experiences," Doblin said from his North Carolina office of the Multidisciplinary Association for Psychedelic Studies, a group he founded. MDMA was already popular among psychotherapists when the government outlawed it. Advocates say it allows people to lower psychological barriers between themselves and others and become less hostile.

'College-aged people have more-prosaic uses for the drug. They often take it alone to dance all night or, in a highly dangerous practice, mix it with LSD, marijuana and alcohol. Ecstasy users say that since 1985, the drug's quality has gone down... The Drug Enforcement Administration has blamed MDMA for 12 deaths in the United States, most stemming from heart failure and accidents. In one case, an ecstasy user tried to climb a live electrical wire. Deaths also have been reported at rave parties in England. Grob said those fatalities probably resulted in part from a lack of oxygen and water in the clubs. Some raves charge as much for water as for alcohol, and turn off the taps in the bathrooms. Dancers experiencing ecstasy's hours-long euphoria can become dehydrated and fall into seizures, he added. Last year, 236 people were rushed to American emergency rooms because of bad reactions to ecstasy.'

MERRY MAN

If one thing is clear, it's that the health ramification of ecstasy use is anything but. I therefore leave the final advice on this subject to the aforementioned pseudonymous correspondent 'Little John', on the grounds that he is *both* clued-up and open-minded: 'If I had to give a flashcard sized piece of advice to users it would be "take 5-htp, don't take more than one dose of MDMA a week (preferably less) and get something to eat/drink before, during, and after." Given this sort of care, I can find no credible evidence or argument that the user will suffer neurotoxic effects. As the person who drinks a beer a day will not damage his liver, the MDMA user that takes a modest dose once a month is extremely unlikely to damage their brain. I suppose the real test is, "would I use MDMA?" And the answer is that I would, I have, and may very well do so again in the future. Whether I understand the risks I'm taking, I leave to the judgment of the reader.'

We still do not know if MDMA causes long-term neurological damage. Consequently, the topic became the bladder wielded – by hysterics, by apologists, by dogmatists and by the emotionally affected – in a great political morris dance. This is the subject of Chapter 5.

05 POLITICS

> 'One young kiddie cried all the water out of his body. Just imagine how his mother felt. And if you're sick on this stuff you can puke your fucking self to death. One girl threw up her own pelvis bone before she snuffed the lid. What a fucking disgrace.'
>
> - Bernard Manning speaking on *Brass Eye*

> 'Just say no to collectivist bullshit.'
>
> - Jason Roth, US journalist

BRASS ATTACKS

Minor celebrities and politicians will spout any old crap to boost their egos. In 1997, UK satirist Christopher Morris took brilliant advantage of this by duping self-righteous 'personalities' to promote entirely fabricated public causes, and incorporating these promotions into his spoof-documentary series *Brass Eye* (UK Channel 4, original air dates 25 January to 9 March 1997). These 'good causes' were not only entirely fabricated, they were patently so. The scenarios were so ludicrous as to make it obvious that these 'celebrities' had no idea of what they spoke, and no authority to say it.

(A back-bench MP acquaintance of mine was approached to appear on a later edition of *Brass Eye* - the now-notorious 'exposé' of paedophilia - and mentioned to me that it was staggeringly obvious that this was a dupe: these researchers were far too nice and accommodating, whereas the usual types are extremely brusque. Politicians need media exposure as the media needs politicians; and the researchers know it.)

For example, the opening programme on animal rights featured 'popular' entertainer/conjuror Paul Daniels and 'Wolf' from *Gladiators* broadcasting heart-rending appeals to assist a baby elephant that had stuck its own trunk up its anus.

Morris's masterpiece was the *Brass Eye* show about drugs. This included such excruciating gems as agony aunt Claire Rayner's disgust at the apparent Japanese practice of smoking cannabis through a dog, and a spoof report about a man who had to sell drugs in order to keep his blind wife in talking books and his disabled teenage daughter in dildos, but the *pièce de résistance* is the fabrication of a new designer drug called 'cake' and the apparent efforts of two supposed pressure groups to combat it. These groups were called Free the United Kingdom from Drugs (FUKD) and British Opposition to Metabolically Bisturbile Drugs (BOMBD). Several television 'personalities' were persuaded to assist FUKD and BOMBD make a promotional film. The result was a prank that showed up both the suspicious motives of personalities prepared to put their public names to 'good causes' and, more generally, the sheer inanity of opinion that forms around emotive subject like ecstasy and the designer drugs based on it.

In this utterly ludicrous scenario, the public figures were made to hold up an individual 'cake' tablet, each indeed about the size of a Victoria sponge but coloured gaudy yellow, and recite nonsensical propaganda and shock stories made up by the *Brass Eye* crew. The astonishing thing was how many supposedly intelligent people, from all spheres of life, believed what they were told to say. They included:

- Bernard Ingham – bluff Yorkshireman, former press secretary to Prime Minister Margaret Thatcher;
- Bernard Manning – obese Mancunian comedian who reckons that jokes at the expense of Asian and Irish people are the essence of humour;
- David Amess – Conservative back-bench MP whom *Brass Eye* duped so successfully that he raised a question on the perils of 'cake' in UK Parliament;

- Rolf Harris – Australian painter and singer who tends to come top in polls when the Great British Public is asked to name an 'artist';
- Jimmy Greaves – ex-genius soccer player/ex-alcoholic pundit;
- Bruno Brookes – ex-Radio 1 disc jockey of the 'old school' who was sacked with a load of other old farts when the station tried to reclaim the 'yoof' audience from commercial radio; and (best of all)
- Noel Edmonds – 'entertainer' who specializes in *Candid Camera*-type japery at the expense of the public and other minor celebrities; never have tables been as comprehensively turned as when a sombre-faced Edmonds was made to speak the immortal words, 'It stimulates the part of the brain known as Shatner's Bassoon.'

This edition of *Brass Eye* is undervalued. It should be shown regularly to expose the ignorant hysteria that emotive subjects unfailingly draw toward themselves. It's this programme that schools should show to impressionable kids if they want to help them decide their future – not 'harrowing' images of dead or dying girls, because they don't work.

DEAD-END KIDS

The images of Leah Betts' and Lorna Spinks' respectively near-dead and dead bodies, attached to respirators in hospital beds and with blood flowing from every facial orifice, certainly shocked contemporary youth into considering and sometimes stopping their ecstasy habits. Temporarily, at least.

Daniel Lennox, who was the Student Union officer at Cambridge's Anglia Polytechnic University's at the time of Lorna Spinks' death, said: 'That put a lot of people off trying [ecstasy] at all… People that had been doing it stopped for quite a long time afterwards because of the shock tactics in the papers.'

A lot of people started up again, though. Shock tactics work in the short term, but people soon repress the shock as a survival mechanism. Moreover, the tactics may well work, but toward the wrong end. Neither Betts nor Spinks was outright killed by MDMA itself (see Chapter 4), but by what they did when they'd taken it.

THE ESSEX GIRL

Leah Betts was the eldest daughter of Paul and Janet Betts and was studying A levels at Basildon College in Essex. She bought the ecstasy tablet that didn't kill her on Saturday 14 October 1995 for £10, after she finished her day job at Alder's department store in Basildon. She consumed it at around 8:30pm that evening whilst celebrating her 18th birthday at a club in Latchindon. Later she told her mother she felt unwell; and collapsed early the following day. Leah's stepmother, Janet Betts, a nurse and a drugs adviser, administered mouth-to-mouth to no avail and Leah fell into a coma. She was taken to Broomfield Hospital in Chelmsford but was never revived. Janet Betts said subsequently, 'She looked stunning that night. She had just blown the candles out and cut the cake. What a waste.'

In his final annual report before he leaves his job, President Clinton's drugs policy adviser, General Barry McCaffrey admitted that America's drugs education and prevention efforts had failed to stem the rising use of ecstasy by the teenagers at whom much of the campaigning was aimed.

Leah's father, Paul Betts, added, 'Just before 1:30am on Sunday she rushed to the bathroom. When she collapsed she screamed for Janet to help her. We could see from her dilated pupils that something was wrong. Jan screamed to her, "What have you taken?" She admitted taking an ecstasy tablet. Her last words before she drifted into a coma were "Help me."'

Paul and Janet Betts allowed photographs of Leah's comatose body be published, as a deterrent to other teenagers against ecstasy. They were very brave to do this: they underwent an experience that is the greatest dread of any parent, whose magnitude non-parents can't even begin to contemplate, and throughout their grief thought of others first. They are still vocal supporters of the anti-drugs movement and they wish to help others learn from their own dreadful experiences. This is the very epitome of unselfishness.

If only they were qualified to do this, it might have just worked. Unfortunately, they aren't – not even Janet Betts, and she's a drugs adviser. There seems to be a public consensus that parents who have faced the tragic bereavement of their children – usually because of murder or else a drugs-related fatality – automatically hold an authoritative voice about how to address the subject.

Some senior policemen agree. Detective Chief Inspector Brian Story of Chelsmsford Police, who handled the Betts inquest, said in a press conference: 'Mr and Mrs Betts are very brave. They are speaking out, and what they are doing will help young people not just locally but across the country.' Many think him wrong.

One of Paul Betts' considered recommendations was that the supplier of the tablet to his daughter should to be hanged. That's not going to happen unless he takes his trade to Thailand. This was grief speaking, not authority. Some argue that people distracted by grief and unable to make a rational decision are really a distraction from reasoned argument, and that emotion should be kept well out of it.

While Leah Betts was still comatose, Paul Betts wrote this open letter to UK parents: 'I feel love for my daughter, anger and hatred for the bastards who supplied her. I thought I knew my own daughter, but does any parent really know where their children are all the time and what they are doing? Children will always be tempted to try something new. In our time it was cigarettes. Today that new experience is drugs. Wherever children are there may be scum like [the suppliers of] these rogue tablets which have probably destroyed my daughter's life. These people prey on our children like vultures and they don't care what their evil trade is doing. Our children must become more aware of the dangers. Drugs are like sex education – a subject to be brushed under the carpet. This can't be right.'

PMA, or paramethoxy-amphetamine, was considered responsible for the death of 18-year-old Chicago woman Sara Aeschlimann in 2000. She died from the collapse of her organs and severe internal bleeding. Her temperature had risen to 42°C (108°F) and authorities described her body as being 'cooked from the inside'. Aeschlimann is thought to have taken seven of the pills. The US Drug Enforcement Administration says that while 'ecstasy is bad, PMA is death'.

Paul Betts' last point is spot on. Drugs must indeed be addressed in schools and escape the same taboo that has prohibited frank sex education lessons and consigned many couples to unwanted pregnancies.

It's the only one of his points that is spot on, though - the rest of his letter is phenomenally wide of the mark.

- The 'bastards', or bastard in singular, who supplied Leah Betts was not some mobster in a seedy dive weighing out drugs on a pair of miniature scales while the whore he pimped for shot smack in the corner. It was more likely one of Betts' close college friends, who would be only marginally less distraught than Paul Betts himself at the tragic consequence of his or her action.
- Children still try cigarettes now. Children tried drugs 'in their days' as well (I don't know when their days were, but children tried drugs during them). In any case, nicotine is a drug .Leah Betts' life wasn't destroyed by a rogue tablet; what she took was uncontaminated MDMA. It was water toxicity that comatized and later killed her (see pp121-2).
- When the letter was written, ecstasy dealers did not 'prey on children like vultures'. MDMA is not an addictive substance and criminal dealers cannot force a habit. Low-level dealers were likely to be entrepreneurial middle-class men, or else young people passing on tablets to their friends.

THE GOLDEN GIRL WHO NEVER GOT TO BE AN OLD WOMAN

Six years later it happened again. Lorna Spinks, a 19-year-old, first-year Sociology student at Anglia Polytechnic University (APU) in Cambridge, was supplied with the ecstasy tablets, which helped to kill her, before she arrived at Cambridge nightclub the Junction. She took two ecstasy tablets and later collapsed because of overheating (see p121): her body temperature increased to 43°C (109°F), three degrees above the safe level, and every organ in her body failed. She died 36 hours later in the intensive care unit of Cambridge's Addenbrookes Hospital.

Lorna Spinks' parents, Alan and Liz, who lived in Cessy, France, had to drive 1,100km (700 miles) through the night to be at their daughter's bedside. Liz Spinks said: 'I knew that things were very bad because the doctors were liaising with us during the journey and asking how long we would be. We realized then that she was critical. They took us to see her and it just wasn't our Lorna.'

If anything, Spinks' parents went even further than those of Betts with their well-meaning shock tactics: they actually conducted interviews in the presence of their daughter's corpse and allowed pictures of it to be published. They wanted every teenager and parent in Britain to look at it. Mrs Spinks explained why they did this: 'I would say to any parent to think about what this family is going through. To see their child look like Lorna, she was so, so pretty and when she was dying she looked like a monster. It looked like she had been run over by a truck. All her organs had been affected. She was bleeding everywhere. They couldn't do anything else and eventually her heart stopped. She's a lovely girl. Her granny called her the Golden Girl, the lovely Lorna. She was very, very popular and had lots of friends.'

She added that they were unaware that their daughter had taken ecstasy in the past, but had since learned from her brother Adrian that she had taken it on occasion.

The pills that helped to kill Lorna Spinks were, in a sense, rogue tablets. They weren't adulterated; rather they were exceptionally strong – an MDMA bumper pack containing twice the usual dosage. This is why the tablets did help to kill her, unlike that taken by Leah Betts, which decidedly did not do so. Spinks, in effect, took four usual doses of MDMA, which when combined with fast dancing amongst heaving bodies packed on a dancefloor, would have caused her body to overheat.

THE UNLUCKY BASTARD WHO GOT CAUGHT

Music student Aaron Strange, aged 19, was found guilty of supplying the ecstasy tablets that helped to kill Spinks, and was given 18 months in a young offenders' institution (two concurrent nine-month sentences after two other attempts to deal ecstasy came to light). Strange was unlucky: he was just in the wrong place at the tragically wrong time, and the people who bought the pills from him were just as guilty as he was. His defence lawyer said that his client was devastated by Lorna's death, and the consequences of what he did would stay with him for the rest of his life.

Moreover, Strange didn't sell the tablets to Spinks herself: he handed them to someone else in her social group. Whoever did pass them on to Spinks was technically a dealer as well.

E-ASY GOING

Alan Spinks was more conciliatory than Paul Betts in his demands for retribution, but he was nevertheless nonplussed at his perceived leniency of Strange's punishment. He said: 'He sold some pills for monetary gain which killed someone and that shouldn't happen. The sentence seems very light. He will probably spend just nine months in a young offenders' institution, which is meant to be a lenient place. I don't feel any great vengeance towards Aaron Strange. He is a very small wheel in a much bigger and more sinister system. However, I do think the powers-that-be have missed an opportunity to show that they are prepared to be strong on drugs. I don't think his life should have been ruined forever but I do think he should have received a lesson and been made an example of.'

Speaking more generally at the original corpse-side interview, Alan Spinks said: 'We would discuss drugs quite openly with Lorna and she said that she wasn't taking anything other than cigarettes and alcohol. I always believed that. So the message is for the parents to be absolutely sure that adolescents come across this stuff.'

Cigarettes and alcohol, of course, are far bigger killers than ecstasy.

CLOSED MINDS

If this easier-going approach mirrored the overall feelings of people connected with the incident – the feelings of Aaron Strange were at least taken into account – the difference between this and the opprobrium spoken by Paul Betts was one of severity, not reasoned opinion. The words were more conciliatory, but the opinions seemed as prejudiced as ever.

APU's communications director, Roy Newson, said: 'Our thoughts must be with the family. What they are going through is beyond imagination and the university will support their efforts to prevent anything of this type happening to any other youngster. At APU, we deplore the illegal use of drugs and our policy is that its use is completely unacceptable.'

Deplore it he may, but accept it he must. Students take drugs - it's practically part of their syllabus. Some university health units refuse to treat anyone who suffers accidents following drink or drug use, so it's no wonder students sometimes snuff it. Offering informed medical or therapeutic assistance to students that have suffered ill drug effects would be far more productive.

NIGHT SPOT ON

Paul Bogen, the director of the nightclub where Lorna Spinks collapsed, was more clued up. He said staff at the Junction had acted swiftly after Lorna collapsed and added: 'On behalf of everyone at the Junction, I offer my extreme condolences to the parents, family and friends of Lorna. The Junction has worked over many years with the police to establish effective procedures for the health and safety of its users. Inevitably, a tragedy like this requires us to review procedures. We do not condone the use of prohibited drugs on or off our premises and will continue to work with the police and relevant agencies to discourage their use.'

That's pretty much spot on. The nature of 'effective procedures' that can help with ecstasy incidents needs to be clarified, though. They necessitate ample water (with clear instructions that it is to be sipped), access to chillout rooms, and one other factor which the Junction, in common with every other UK nightclub, won't have - a drugs professional located inside the club who can check ecstasy for rogue tablets.

AMERICAN DIE

Ecstasy fatalities do happen in the USA. They're relatively uncommon, but they do happen.

JILLIAN KIRKLAND

Jillian Kirkland died in August 1998 after taking ecstasy at a rave in the State Palace Theater in New Orleans. After 16 days in intensive care at Charity Hospital, Jillian died at the age of 17. Her mother apparently still makes a four-hour trip every day to visit her daughter's grave. When interviewed, she chokes and recalls Jillian as 'only 17, a beautiful 17'.

BRITNEY CHAMBERS

Britney Chambers of Denver, Colorado, collapsed on her 16th birthday on 27 January 2001. She was given the clover-leaf-embossed pill that didn't kill her by friends at Monarch High School in Louisville and took it at her mother's house later that day. Misinformation killed Britney Chambers: she knew that ecstasy had dehydrating effects but hadn't heard of water toxicity so she drank 13.5 litres (24 pints) of water within 45 minutes and fell into a coma when her brain cells swelled up like sponges. By Friday she had been brain dead for several days and her family gave permission for doctors to take her off life support.

TRAVIS SCHUEGER

Police arrested 20-year-old Travis Schueger, along with his 18-year-old girlfriend Rebecca Sheffield, on suspicion of distributing the pill, and bail was set for $7,500 (£5,200) and $2,500 (£1,700) respectively. They arrested four juvenile girls in the same case, who faced felony charges of distribution of a controlled substance.

SHOCK TACTICS

This is an extract from the *Guardian* of 3 March 2002 commenting on the release of pictures of the corpse of heroin addict Rachel Whitear, who fatally overdosed on 10 May 2000:

> *Shock campaigns against drug use are not new. Neither are concerns about their efficacy. A report to the Teachers Advisory Council on Alcohol and Drug Education in 1986 criticized such tactics and pointed out they had failed in other areas.*
>
> *The 1950s [actually, 1936] educational film* Reefer Madness *was intended to shock American youngsters into avoiding cannabis. Instead, it helped to create the image of cannabis as cool and desirable and became a cult classic.*
>
> *In the mid-1980s, the government responded to a surge in heroin use with a television and poster campaign featuring a wasted youth with the caption: 'Heroin screws you up.' Dozens of posters went*

missing as the boy in them became a teenage pin-up. Within months 'heroin chic' appeared on the catwalks.

Three years ago, a video called The Trap *featuring real addicts and a staged overdose was shown to 11-year-olds at 50 primary schools in the Rhondda Valley, South Wales. The area still has a massive heroin problem.*

More recently, the Leah Betts poster campaign, featuring her photograph under the headline 'Sorted – Just one ecstasy tablet killed Leah Betts', was quickly hijacked by the pro-ecstasy lobby, who released a rival poster: 'Distorted – You are just as likely to die from eating a bay leaf as from an ecstasy tablet.'

According to Neil Hunt, lecturer in addictive behaviours at the University of Kent, a film with images of Leah Betts is so often shown in schools that some children 'take the mickey out of it'.

The video of Rachel's addiction and death was made by Hereford local education authority. In addition to graphic pictures of her corpse, it features interviews with her parents and her best friend.

'It makes teachers and parents feel better, but the actual value is highly questionable,' said Hunt. 'Videos like this allow schools to tick the "drugs education" box and feel that they have done what they need to do. Actually talking to schoolchildren about heroin – a drug they are very unlikely to be exposed to – as opposed to tobacco or alcohol – which they almost certainly will be – doesn't make sense.'

Harry Shapiro of the agency Drugscope said heroin use was often due to psychological or social problems that a short video wasn't going to address.

For some, however, the controversy detracts from the real issues.

'At the end of the day, this woman's daughter died,' says Chris Smart, who made the film. 'After that, nothing else matters.'

The following day's *Guardian* featured this letter from Richard Ives: 'The anti-drugs video showing the shocking image of the dead Rachel Whitear was made to scare young people so that they don't use drugs. It seems common sense, but the evidence is against it. In another area of prevention, a recent research review of scare tactics aimed at juvenile delinquents has shown that they do not work. In the US, "scared straight" programmes take teenagers into prisons to frighten them into avoiding crime. A systematic review of several evaluations of these programmes concludes that (in the words of a summary) "scared straight-like programmes not only are ineffective but are likely to increase crime and delinquency." As you report there is no evidence that the Leah Betts video reduced ecstasy use. Neither will the Rachel Whitear video reduce heroin use. Tackling drugs problems requires more thoughtful approaches. We must not follow the tabloid tendency to focus on the extremes of young people's drug use when the experience of the average drug-using teenager is so different – and so often enjoyable. We have to start with young people's perspectives and be rigorous in our assessment of our interventions; only then will we have a chance of influencing their behaviour and reducing drug-related deaths.'

HYST-E-RIA

When a topic like ecstasy – a drug whose true qualities are relatively unknown to scientists, let alone the tabloid-buying public – hits the news, the resulting hysteria can produce consequences that are both ill considered and borderline dangerous. Governments are pressurized to introduce rushed legislation that singularly fails to address the real issues, while the drug users themselves rebel against this authoritarianism and therefore miss out on potentially life-saving advice.

AMERICA'S LEAST WANTED

Brits don't have the monopoly on drugs hysteria. The American public is pretty darn good at it too. They have to be, otherwise President Clinton wouldn't have appointed Barry McCaffrey as drugs tsar.

One presumes that Clinton took his time to think about this appointment, that he considered experts in fields germane to reasoned debate on drugs policy – social workers, say, or probation officers, or medics or psychiatrists. When he appointed McCaffrey, he knew was good at his job. His achievements spoke for themselves.

- He was twice awarded the Distinguished Service Cross, America's second highest valour award.
- He received three Purple Heart medals for wounds received in combat. He was commander of the 24th Mechanized Infantry Division, Operation Desert Storm.
- He served as the assistant to General Colin Powell and supported the chairman as the JCS adviser to the Secretary of State and the US ambassador to the United Nations.
- He was the most highly decorated and youngest four-star general in the US Army.

The fact that his job was that of Army General, and that he knew sod all about drugs, was of trifling concern.

DARK TSAR

Maybe only public hysteria could have induced Clinton to appoint a militaristic public hero as drugs tsar. Open minds and reasoned debate - attributes entirely necessary for a drugs tsar - are conversely rather dangerous in military leaders lest the boys start revolting and demanding bigger rations and softer toilet paper.

Clinton wanted to appoint someone perceptible as a leader. Whether he led in the right direction was of lesser consequence. It's the sort of topsy-turvy scenario that W S Gilbert would lampoon were he alive today (and if he could find a rhyme for 'methamphetamine').

In February 2001 a Dutch man was arrested, charged and later jailed for attempting to smuggle ecstasy into the USA by swallowing 3,500 pills with a street value of £45,000 ($65,000).

Here McCaffrey writes of his role models. This is hardly the stuff of a man who can emphasize with desperate addicts living on sink estates (I've purposefully not edited this quotation, based on the suspicion that a policy-maker who doesn't know the real deals about possessive apostrophes and ellipses isn't going anywhere fast): 'The real influences on my early career were NCO's... my first 82nd Abn Plt Sgt Comar Johnson and the 1st Sgt...my Vietnam Co 1Sgt Emerson Trainer....one of the three Bn CSM's who worked for me... my Bde CSM who went on to be SGM of the Army...and my Div CSM during Desert Storm. Also several US NCO's who tutored me as a Lt and Cpt in the Viet Abn Div. From these terrific soldiers, I learned the culture of the Army, standards, personal field competence, and I fell in love with the Field Army.'

McCaffrey was probably well meaning in his actions, but his simplistic and dogmatic approach to the job was only matched by his manipulative sentimentality. Notoriously he used to flaunt a bracelet during television interviews; when he was invited to explain why he was wearing a women's adornment, McCaffrey's eyes would well up as he explained how it was passed on to him by the parents of a 12-year-girl whose young life was cut short by heroin.

DUTCH UMBRAGE

McCaffrey's 1998 fact-finding visit to Amsterdam – where he soundly pissed off his Dutch hosts by refusing to find any facts that didn't accord with his dogmas – should have sounded an extended cautionary note, beginning when he stepped off the plane on to Dutch soil and ending on a strangled tone when he landed back in Washington. McCaffrey dropped sufficient gaffes to leave Prince Philip looking like Henry Kissinger in comparison. Here are some diplomatic gems, McCaffrey-style:

- He warned Dutch authorities they were 'putting American children at risk' with their relaxed laws on marijuana;
- He accused The Netherlands of producing half of Europe's amphetamines and much of its MDMA;
- He criticized Holland's coffee-shop culture, where customers can purchase Colombian hashish to match their coffee;
- He slated The Hague's heroin maintenance programme, which provides registered addicts with good-quality heroin.

The Dutch, for some reason, didn't quite hit it off with McCaffrey. Holland's health minister, Els Borst, said that McCaffrey refused to accept the facts on the results of Dutch drugs policy that he was presumably there to find out. She added that, in her opinion, America's draconian drugs policy didn't stop young people from experimenting. Of McCaffrey's unresponsiveness she said: 'When I say we prefer they only experiment with cannabis, he just falls silent and gazes ahead.'

The Dutch health ministry doubted whether his visit had any purpose. A spokesman said: 'He should get his ideas more in tune with reality.'

LOCAL ZERO

McCaffrey didn't believe there was a national drugs problem in the US so much as a series of community epidemics, which each locality must tackle separately. In other words he bred parochialism, and drafted in all levels of government (federal, state and local), non-governmental organizations, the private sector and individual citizens to propagate distrust. Extracts from a report of 28 April 2000 indicates this seeming simplicity with clarity.

> *'The magnitude of the drug problem in this country is enormous,' says Barry McCaffrey, director of the Office of National Drug Control Policy within the White House, the coordination point for the many U.S. government programs that attempt to deal with one or another aspect of the problem. According to McCaffrey, drugs are responsible for the deaths of 52,000 Americans a year, and the cost of the problem adds up to $110 billion [£76 billion] a year. Like any complex social issue, however, the 'drug problem,' when viewed up close, has many facets. In a sense it is many problems, a series of community epidemics.*
>
> *'But the drug problem is also an international problem – one that requires, as the current National Drug Control Strategy makes clear, a multi-pronged international approach. Thus domestic efforts to reduce demand for drugs in the United States and treatment programs available to drug addicts work together with efforts to control borders and U.S.-funded efforts to interdict drug shipments abroad.*
>
> *'We are not confronting a national drug problem, but a series of community epidemics. Our hope for reducing drug use lies in confronting the needs of each locality, one community at a time.*
>
> *'The most effective strategies for preventing drug use, keeping drugs out of neighborhoods and schools, and providing a safe and*

secure environment for all people are co-operative efforts that mobilize and involve all elements of a community.'

MAD CAMPAIGN

Accordingly, McCaffrey set up a $5 million (£3.5 million) radio and Internet campaign targeted at youths in 106 US radio markets. This was escalated to a $1 billion (£700,000) all-media campaign that saturated US airwaves with shock-tactic advertisements and the worldwide web with pop-up banners. His intentions were, in his own words: 'to educate and enable America's youth to reject illegal drugs as well as alcohol and tobacco. Using realistic portrayals of the consequences of drug use, the Media Campaign shows the harmful effects of drugs and the benefits of a drug-free lifestyle. It also "denormalizes" drug use by reminding people that most youth do not use drugs, and it empowers parents with information and strategies to keep their children drug-free. We've got to talk to parents who are taking their young people to an all-night rave and seeing police uniforms and believing that because it's quoted as alcohol-free that this is a safe environment. Their young people are at risk in that environment.'

BANNER IN THE WORKS

McCaffrey got weaving and came up with the following:

- Anti-ecstasy radio ads placed in radio stations in 106 markets across the country;
- Internet banner advertisements about ecstasy added to websites popular with young people;
- The key words 'ecstasy', 'MDMA', 'club drugs' and others being bought by the campaign to monopolize Internet search engines (in other words, when people did an Internet search on 'ecstasy' – irrespective of whether they were chemists looking for an MDMA recipe or students researching 'the sublime in romantic English verse' – they would get one of Barry McCaffrey's banners);
- The pop-up banners directed readers to one of two websites, intended for youth and parents respectively. These are still going 'strong' (never

have inverted commas been so necessary) and may incline readers either to laugh or vomit, though hopefully not both.

YOUNG-WAGGING

The youth site www.freevibe.com carries the risible tone of a trendy 30-something schoolteacher trying to identify with the kids. It is an attempt at a teenage magazine replete with agony aunts, letters pages and star interviews, but instead of dating advice and fashion guides it slants every feature toward the simplistic 'Just say no' drugs approach devised by Nancy Reagan during the 1980s and still beloved of anti-drug pressure groups. The current 'issue', for example, includes this letter from a teenager that I have deliberately not edited: 'The worst thing that could happen to you in your life is probly what i have most likly been through. Drugs and alchohal are the worst things.i had this friend her aka is shortie ahe used to be against drinking N SMOKiN and Goofy and Brat and me.We were all against it until we started to hang out with boys that have been doing this stuff for a while.Then we got into all of that and that was over the summer of last year i had just got out of the eighth grade and was doing this all summer long all day and night long.hten when it cam around to school we did it every weekend.Ny grades were nad and i didnt care.All i cared about was the weekend so i could do it all over again.Then when i got caught i stoped i was so werid like i didnt fell normal when i got caught and had to stop But i did and now i dont talk to those gurls anymore because i wasent alowed back there and i started to hang out with some new people and they dont talk to me for that.They got mad when i told them that i quit doing that.i only saw then a few weeks ago at the mall when i went to go and get pictures done and Aka Brat she looked so bad.So looked unhealthy and soo tired and looked parinoied and anxiouse and she looked really nasty. AND know one should end up like that i hope they can stop and get better because i have and i fell better and like my own self and i fell alot mosr prettier i dont fell like i m so high that i need so much make up to make me look better and not tired and not disgusting.im alot more happier now then i was.Truthfully i did like the high i was on for about seven months but now i know it was a waste of my life.'

This young lady's priority would appear to be basic literacy, not drugs education. She'll waste far less of her life if she learns to write.

The star interview in the issue is conducted by resident interviewer 'Kenji' with *Sabrina The Teenage Witch*'s Melissa Joan Hart. It concludes with the truly cryptic Q and A:

Kenji: What is your Anti Drug?

MJH: My sisters.

Kenji: Thanks so much for your time.'

Quite how that offers a constructive drugs message to the 'yoof' is beyond me, however.

BANNERED TO THE TOP SHELF

McCaffrey's adult site www.theantidrug.com tells parents how to bring up their kids in a manner that accords the word 'patronizing' a whole new vista of meaning. The site is offered, in true imperialist fashion, in Spanish, Cambodian, Chinese, Korean and Vietnamese translations. The tone of the site is unrelentingly dogmatic – for example, parents teaching their kids about marijuana are advised to adopt the following approach: 'Some parents who saw marijuana being widely used in their youth still wonder, "Is marijuana really so bad for my child?" The answer is an emphatic "Yes!"'

Wrong. The real answer is a less than emphatic 'Erm...don't know. But it's certainly safer than alcohol.'

The media is correctly vilified by the site, but for the wrong reasons: again the approach is overly dogmatic, and it takes everything out of context. For example, the logical extension of its cinema guide is that on no account should children be allowed to see such subversive material as Disney's *Dumbo* or Chaplin's *Modern Times* because 'if you laugh at a drunk or stoned person in a movie, you may be sending the wrong message to your child. Be a role model – the person you want your kid to be. What stronger anti-drug message is there?'

HAPP-E FAMILIES

The family, of course, is the building block from which society is built, unless it happens to be presided over by a single mother or – horror of horrors – a couple of homosexuals, in which case it should be resigned to the scrap heap. So speaks Middle England and Bible Belt America, the latter of which constitutes www.theantidrug.com's intended readership. What follows is its advice for those all-important regular family get-togethers. (If you're a single parent living in a slum apartment, then tough.)

- *Kids who are close to their parents are the least likely to engage in risky behaviors. The more involved you are in your children's lives, the more valued they'll feel, and the more likely they'll be to respond to you. Try to schedule regular get-togethers with your children.*
- *Establish 'together time.' Keep a regular time each week for doing something special with your child – even if it's just going out for ice cream. Even a few minutes of conversation while you're cleaning up after dinner or right before bedtime can help the family catch up and establish the open communication that is essential to raising drug-free children.*
- *Have family meetings. Held regularly at a mutually agreed upon time, family meetings provide a forum for discussing triumphs, grievances, projects, questions about discipline, and any topic of concern to a family member. Ground rules help. Everyone gets a chance to talk; one person talks at a time without interruption; everyone listens; and only positive, constructive feedback is allowed. To get resistant children to join in, combine the get-together with incentives such as post-meeting pizza or assign them important roles such as recording secretary or rule enforcer.*
- *Don't be afraid to ask where your kids are going, who they'll be with, and what they'll be doing. Get to know your kids' friends – and their parents – so you're familiar with their activities.*

- *Try to be there after school. The 'danger zone' for drug use is between 4 and 6pm. Arrange flexitime at work if you can. If your child will be with friends, make sure there's adult supervision, not just an older sibling.*
- *Eat meals together as often as you can. Meals are a great opportunity to talk about the day's events, to unwind, reinforce and bond. Studies show that kids whose families eat together at least five times a week are less likely to be involved with drugs or alcohol.*

ACT YOUR AGE

Of course, all work and no play makes J Jack Junior a dull boy, so the site also suggests playtime activities, which include this feast-of-fun role-playing game about 'peer pressure':

> *Here is a potential role-playing scenario for you to try with your daughter (You can turn the scenario around for your boys, or come up with other scenarios that fit the same pattern - anything to get your children to practise their own resistance skills):*
>
> *Take the role of a boy she likes and try to persuade her to share a six-pack of beer with you. What can she say? 'You're such a jerk!' is alienating. 'I don't know...' leaves the door open and sounds like she could be coaxed. The middle ground, in which she's firm but friendly, works best. Help her rehearse key phrases that give reasons for why she simply won't have a beer:*
>
> - *'My parents would kill me if they found out, and they always find out!'*
> - *No, I'm not into that stuff.'*
> - *'I tried it once, and I hate the taste.'*
> - *'My parents trust me to not drink, and I don't want to break that trust.'*

Or she could state the consequences of drinking:

- *'I tried it once and ended up vomiting on everything!'*
- *'Drinking would make me feel out of control, and I hate that.'*

She'll need to be prepared for protests. She can meet them with the 'broken record' technique, in which she repeats her reason for not drinking over and over until attempts at persuading her cease. Or she can make it clear that the discussion about beer is over by changing the subject:

- *'Did you watch the basketball game last night?' or*
- *'Hey, do you know if that concert's sold out?'*

If all else fails, she should leave the scene, saying, 'I've got to go.'

WE DON'T NEED NO DRUGS EDUCATION

Educators aren't forgotten, however. That rare breed of teachers who like to be told how to do their job can benefit from pre-prepared lesson plans such as this essential learning activity focusing on how to advertise against drugs:

1. *Introduce the activity by discussing the fact that people are influenced by many factors, including their families, peers, teachers, etc. Another big influence on individuals is the media (TV, radio, CDs, the Internet) – especially advertising. Explain that in this activity students will create their own anti-drug advertisements to share with others.*
2. *Discuss with students that although the purpose of most advertising strategies is to sell a product or service, other advertising strategies are designed to send a particular message. Ask students:*

    - *Can you think of examples of advertising that try to sell a product or service? (Examples may include soda, cereal, medicine, diet programs, tax assistance, etc.)*

- *Can you think of examples of ads that send a message? (eg, political-related ads, literacy ads, anti-drug ads, etc)*

3 *Discuss that advertising can occur through the use of different mediums, such as print, radio, TV, or even web pages (called banners). Using more than one medium helps for two reasons: (a) to expose more people to the advertisements, and (b) to get people to hear the same message many times.*

4 *Explain that this activity is related to a real anti-drug advertising campaign whose purpose is sending a message to people about the dangers of drug use, ways to help prevent drug use among young people, and the positive consequences of remaining drug-free. Ask if students can remember recently seeing any advertisements sending anti-drug messages.*

5 *Explain to students that for this activity, their anti-drug ads should focus on one of the following approaches:*

- *Positive consequences – show the positive consequences that can be achieved from living a drug-free life. (Example: performing well in sports or making good grades in school.)*
- *Resistance strategies – show ways teens can resist pressure to use drugs. (Example: Walk away.)*

Make sure not all students select the same message.

6 *Show students examples of ads from 'Resistance Strategies' Anti-drug Ads for Teens and/or 'Positive Consequences' Anti-drug Ads for Teens. If Internet access is not available, print ads can be printed off ahead of time and can be shown alone (many of the print ads are related to some of the TV and radio ads, so students can still get an idea of different ads). For each example shown, ask students which approach is being used? Who is the target audience for each ad?*

7 *Divide students into small groups of three to four students (for*

Art classes you may want students to work on their print ads individually). Explain that each group will be designing their own anti-drug ad.

8 *Distribute 'Planning a PSA/Anti-drug Ad' Worksheet to each group (or student). Each group will use the worksheet to plan their ad and decide important factors such as:*

- *Which type of ad (print, radio, TV, or web-based)? (Modify choices depending on subject area)*
- *Which of the two approaches will be used?*
- *Who is the target audience?*

9 *Explain your criteria and guidelines to students, tell them the length for TV and radio ads is 30 seconds, and that they need to develop a script. For print ads, use poster-sized paper, no smaller than 12" X 17" [30 x 43cm]. If you have the capability to publish ads in a local newspaper or publication, follow the appropriate guidelines for those venues. In addition, make sure any health information included is current and the message persuasive and passionate. Give examples. (These criteria can be used to assess PSAs for grading.)*

10 *Have students discuss elements of persuasive communications and what they mean. Allow time for students to plan and draft their anti-drug advertisements. Approve students' drafts for appropriateness before they complete their final products. If students need to research background information (including drug facts) for their ads, have them log on to www.freevibe.com, a website for teens which includes drug facts.*

11 *After approval, students should continue completing their ads and rehearsing if necessary. If resources are available, videotape or audiotape TV and radio ads. Otherwise, have groups/students present their anti-drug ads to the rest of the class. Debrief after each ad presentation to discuss the approach used, the intended target audience, and any comments or suggestions that*

observers may have. For fun, have students vote on their two favorite ads.

JUST 'JUST SAY NO'

Experienced teachers know that that's a crock of the proverbial: kids don't like to be pulled a fast one, and that particular 'one' is positively supersonic. That's why sex education moved on leaps and bounds (for adventurous couples) when it progressed beyond 'Don't do that: you'll go blind/get pregnant' to 'Don't do that: but if you *do* do it, here's how we can help'. In other words, current sex education recommends abstinence, but nonetheless offers contraception and STD advice to those who do choose to have sex. Kids respect that. They catch on that educationalists are being honest, and leaving their informed sexual choices in their own (or partner's if they're lucky) hands.

Drugs education should follow the same principles: advise kids to 'Just say no' to drugs, but also offer unbiased information and useful advice to those who take up a habit. It should also tell kids that some drugs, and drug-taking methods, are more dangerous than others are.

McCaffrey and the US Congress just said no to this. Money earmarked for drug education was strictly limited to abstinence-only programmes. It's an approach that kills people, but at least it appeases the undecided voters at election time.

Joel Brown, director of the Center for Educational Research and Development, writes:

> *Our research, along with numerous other studies, shows that young people experience a significant emotional disturbance when their educational experience doesn't match their real life experience in regards to drugs. The challenges they face are much more complex than just being able to say no to drugs. Eventually they must learn to be responsible decision makers with regards to prescription drugs, alcohol, tobacco and other drugs. So the information they receive is not only insufficient, it ill prepares them for the challenging and complex drug decisions that they will face over their lives.*

SORTING THE WHEAT FROM THE MCCAFFREY

McCaffrey's websites do contain some useful advice – it would be unfair to infer that they don't. For example, www.theantidrug.com entreats parents to reward their children's successes and keep any punishment for their misdemeanours minor – which is exactly correct. The problem is that their tone is so relentlessly paternalist and patronizing that 'preaching to the converted' doesn't do it justice. Anyone that really matters will take one look, laugh or vomit, then move on.

HIGHS, DAMNED HIGHS AND STATISTICS

Objective research tended to show that the campaign had made not a jot of difference, even though McCaffrey reckoned that it had worked a treat. President Clinton agreed with him, too, as indeed he had to in order to save whatever of his face still remained. 'If you're a teenager or parent it is nearly impossible to avoid seeing or hearing our anti-drug messages on television or radio several times a week,' the President smugly proclaimed.

JEST EXPANDERS

In 1998 Clinton and McCaffrey duly expanded the media campaign for another five years on a national basis, upping the cost to a massive $1 billion (£700,000). The White House's press office explained how they would implement this.

NATIONAL YOUTH E-ATURE

Begun as a 12-city pilot, the National Youth Anti-Drug Media Campaign was expanded to Phase II in July 1998 by President Clinton. White House publicists wrote:

> EXPANDING THE CAMPAIGN'S REACH
>
> *Today, the President released an evaluation of Phase II, showing that it has surpassed expectations and is successfully changing youth attitudes and alerting our kids to the dangers of drugs. The evaluation showed:*

- *The Campaign has exceeded its goal of reaching 90 per cent of target audiences at a frequency of 4-7 times a week;*
- *The percentage of youth claiming that the ads 'made them stay away from drugs' rose from 61 to 69 per cent;*
- *The percentage of youth reporting that they 'learned a lot about the drugs from the ads' rose from 44 to 55 per cent.*

President Clinton unveiled new components of Phase III of the Campaign, including:

- *New television and radio ads with new messages designed for target audiences;*
- *New public-private partnerships that will generate a wide range of coordinated anti-drug activities with schools, civic organizations, community anti-drug coalitions, and others.*

OTHER STRATEGIES

- Eighty-two different adverts presented via television, radio, newspapers, magazines, the Internet, bus stops, subway cars, movie screens and video games;
- Yet more teaching materials provided to teachers;
- After-school activities organized by the YMCA;
- A new 'brand', the Anti-Drug, to symbolize the campaign.
- 'We're trying to be where the young kids are,' said McCaffrey.

MAY THE REMORSE BE WITH YOU

The idea – inspired of all things by the blanket coverage of the *Star Wars* films – was to swamp America's youth into anti-drugs submission. The target was for 90 per cent of US teens to see four anti-drug messages a week.

Again, McCaffrey reckoned he'd come up trumps. He said: 'The percentage of youth who said they were scared of taking drugs increased during the evaluation period. Teens said that the four ads targeted to their age group made them less likely to try or use drugs.'

Clinton concurred again:

We expected the ads would greatly increase awareness. What we didn't expect was that the ads would already have a measurable effect on attitudes. This is a very good sign. What it proves is, I suppose, what we should have known all along, that if advertising works in commerce and advertising works in politics, advertising ought to work on this issue as well.

The findings – including the results of national school-based surveys of youth in grades 4 through 12, a national telephone survey of parents, and the results of site visits in 12 communities across the country – indicate that the Media Campaign is having a pronounced influence on our nation's youth and families. These findings, in fact, are similar to those from Phase I, demonstrating that the Campaign is meeting its goal of increasing awareness, which is the first step in changing attitudes and behaviors. Among the major findings of the most recent evaluation:

- *The paid placement of anti-drug advertisements brought significant increases in awareness of Campaign ads and messages among all age groups and key ethnic groups;*
- *The ads proved highly effective. The number of youth who agreed that the ads made them 'stay away from drugs' increased a substantial eight percentage points between baseline study and follow-up;*
- *The number of youth who agreed that the ads told them something they didn't know about drugs increased 8.2 percent.*

A MAN WHO DOESN'T NEED DRUGS TO GET SPACED

On 13 September 1999, McCaffrey joined second-man-on-the-moon Buzz Aldrin to address students from Stuart-Hobson Middle School to introduce a youth drug prevention area on NASA's website.

The idea was to develop an extensive information network involving hundreds of websites and chatrooms across the Internet, targeting youth, parents and other significant adults. NASA was the first US government

Glowsticks being sold at the Glastonbury Festival, 2000.

An E'd-up raver wielding glowsticks. The shining tubes are reported to bring on the euphoric state associated with ecstasy.

agency to place irrelevant anti-drug links on its websites as part of this National Youth Anti-Drug Media Campaign.

Aldrin said, 'For young people who want to follow in my footsteps, on the moon, you have to be drug-free. Explore space, not drugs.'

McCaffrey proved a dab hand at making 'spaced out'/'literally in space' comparisons himself: 'If your dream is to reach the stars, you can't get there by getting high. Through participation in the website initiative, NASA is serving as a leader in the campaign to keep America's youth drug-free. It is critical that all of us in the government and private sectors do everything possible to send this strong message to kids. An important part of this Campaign's strategy is to surround youth with drug-free messaging, wherever they spend their time, especially in locations where it might not be expected.'

The drug prevention area of the NASA website takes 'patronizing' to the highest possible standpoint. It includes:

- clean-living quotes from astronauts;
- electronic postcards with anti-drug messages;
- information about the negative effects of specific drugs;
- games;
- entertaining links – in NASA's own words, 'to keep kids coming back'.

Its intention was 'to emphasize that illicit drug use harms the mental, physical and social skills [of kids] needed to become an astronaut or work for NASA'.

NASA was the first of 19 government agencies to sully their websites like this – either with the all-out 'drugs and games' separate section, or just including one of Barry's banners.

BILL'S AND BARRY'S BOLLOCKS

McCaffrey and Clinton claimed that data from teen questionnaires revealed that the advertisements were very successful at the national level:

> *There was a dramatic 59.3 per cent increase in the number of teens who 'agree a lot' that the 'Frying Pan' ad [a US public-information film portraying a skillet-wielding girl smashing an egg and her whole*

> *kitchen then used as a supposed metaphor for heroin use] made them less likely to try or use drugs (rising from 23 to 36 percent).The survey results also indicated that parent audiences found the advertising informative. Parents stated that the ads gave them a better understanding of the problems of drug use in young people.*

Others disagreed. 'How about a campaign that encourages stupid, apathetic morons not to fuck until they feel like actually raising a kid?' is the ironic comment of US journalist Jason Roth. He doesn't take a pro-drugs stance, but rather insists that the slant of drugs education should be toward people taking responsibility for their lives, and that drugs merely allow them to escape this responsibility. In his opinion, an effective drugs campaign must comprise, to paraphrase his words:

- a campaign that emphasizes the importance of self-esteem and individual responsibility;
- a campaign that reinforces the importance of reality, the need to be conscious of it and the fact that drugs prevent you from doing so;
- a campaign that talks about the importance of using your own mind to identify reality and make some attempt to deal with it;
- a campaign that says maybe it's all right if kids are eccentric or individualist, just as long as they understand the importance of setting goals, thinking for themselves and making their own decisions.

Roth asserts that the McCaffreyite media campaign is grossly counterproductive, in effect encouraging kids to increase their drug taking as an act of revolt against McCaffrey, and also destroying confidence of kids by labelling them as 'losers', and therefore likely to make kids take up drugs as an escape from reality. He maintains that the media campaigns of McCaffrey and others have 'spouted their pseudo-moralistic bullshit' in such a way that:

- wastes millions of taxpayers' dollars;
- allays guilt of capitalist advertisers and consumers by showing advertising agents seemingly acting selflessly for the good of all;

- gives counterproductive messages about drug use;
- talks down to people in the most self-righteous tone possible.

THE TOUCHABLES

Some detractors of McCaffrey reckon that the anti-drugs measures have the opposite effect to that intended - that what is in effect 'prohibition' of drugs conversely gives kids more access to drugs. This is likened to the prohibition of alcohol during the 1920s in the United States, which federal government ostensibly brought about to protect children from misuse of alcohol, but eventually had to repeal for exactly the same reason.

A 1998 survey of US high-school children suggested that what McCaffrey termed a 'drugs war' conversely made drugs *easier* to obtain. Kids like to play soldiers, after all. Students reckoned that banned narcotic substances were easier to obtain (for those under the US age limit of 21) than banned alcoholic ones. The poll revealed that, in the kids' experience:

- marijuana was 'fairly easy' to obtain;
- cocaine was 'easily' available;
- ecstasy was 'easily' available;
- LSD was 'easily" available.

LEGAL DEFENDER

The obvious conclusion, say pro-legalization groups, is that all drugs should be legalized and therefore placed under government control. This of course should be beneficial to federal and local government, because they could levy taxes on the drugs while keeping the prices high as a deterrent to people starting a drugs habit or an incentive for them to give one up - thus killing two birds with one stonehead.

Conversely, in a black market drugs are becoming ever more available and ever less expensive as market forces come into play (see p72). McCaffrey turned his coke-free nose up at that: 'American parents clearly don't want children to use a fake ID at the corner store to buy heroin.'

The pro-legalizers' comeback to that pearl of wisdom was that black-market drugs dealers tend not to require any ID, fake or otherwise.

COUNTER SCHLOCK-WISE

Kevin Zeese, president of Common Sense for Drug Policy (CSDP), said that McCaffrey's advertising campaigns were profoundly counterproductive:

> *General McCaffrey clearly preferred funding TV commercials to investing in America's youth. We are spending nearly twice as much on the ad campaign, the glittering jewel in his drug-war crown, than the federal government spends on after-school programs for kids, even though research shows alternative activity programs to be the most effective way to prevent adolescent drug abuse... Barry McCaffrey says that we are turning the corner in our fight against drugs. If that's true, then American parents ought to be very concerned about what horrors are lurking around that corner.*

DRUGS TSAR LESS THAN ECSTATIC

McCaffrey seemed to be especially one-sided in his treatment of ecstasy. None of the following statement of his is proven:

> *[Ecstasy] is not a safe drug. This is a powerful and destructive substance that can wreck mind and body. Ecstasy destroys serotonin-producing neurons and reduces serotonin, a neurotransmitter involved in controlling mood, sleep, pain, sexual activity, and violent behavior... MDMA causes long-lasting damage to areas of the brain critical for thought and memory... People who take MDMA even just a few times will likely have long-term, perhaps permanent, problems with learning and memory.*

At least that statement of his is only unproven. This one's plain inaccurate:

> *In my judgment, ecstasy is the fastest growing drug problem among teens. I don't think we've reached the end of the curve yet. I think we're still on an uphill climb as to the level of damage it's going to do in our society. One of the reasons for that is there is so much misleading information about this drug.*

I had the opportunity to go to Denver, Colorado, to announce the arrest and prosecution of about 30 individuals in an ecstasy distribution ring. The case started out on the 16th birthday of Britney Chambers. On her birthday, one of her friends gave her an ecstasy pill that killed her. Local law enforcement arrested the perpetrator that distributed that pill. But the DEA was able to get back to the organization that brought those pills into the country, and even back to the original source in the Netherlands. What was troubling to me was that after Britney Chambers died, headlines in the newspapers read 'Tainted ecstasy Kills Teen.' The news story made it seem that ecstasy alone wasn't enough to kill, only if it was tainted. The fact is in Britney's case, it wasn't tainted. It was pure ecstasy. This is the kind of knowledge gap we're up against – the belief that ecstasy is somehow safe.

It may have been pure ecstasy, but it didn't kill her. Water toxicity did. This might be a suitable juncture to repeat the refrain from Chapter 4: ecstasy does not kill.

DESPERATE DISPLEASURES

Unsurprisingly, McCaffrey's measures to combat ecstasy were draconian at best, and grossly counterproductive at worst.

This is illustrated by consequences following the aforementioned death of Jillian Kirkland. Contemporary reports wrongly attributed her collapse to 'a lethal dosage of MDMA' and panic measures ensued, spurred on by alarmist newspaper reports and editorials like this one from *The Times-Picayune* of 30 August 2000:

Devotees of raves talk about the sound of loud electronic music that's irresistible to young dancers. They talk about the lights, from the elaborate laser displays to the glow sticks that they swing around the dance floor. They talk about the ethos: peace, love, unity.

What they are less eager to talk about is the drugs.

But drug use is part of the phenomenon. And while not every young person whose social life revolves around the all-age, all-night dance parties uses them, designer drugs are inextricably linked to the rave scene. [Actually, ecstasy hasn't been a designer drug since it became illegal.]

Just ask emergency room personnel. They know when a big party is on in New Orleans, because they see the casualties: 23 brought into the Charity Hospital emergency room for drug-related problems after a rave at the State Palace Theater last month and another five last weekend. It's typical to see an ambulance posted outside rave venues, too.

The toll from last weekend's rave included a minor who is in guarded condition at Charity after suffering seizures, kidney failure and a 106°F [41°C] temperature. Although doctors expect him to survive, his case is frighteningly reminiscent of 17-year-old Jillian Kirkland, an Alabama girl who died here in 1998 from drug overdose complications. She was in convulsions for more than an hour on the dance floor of the State Palace Theater before she was taken to the hospital, where she died several weeks later... Getting rid of the drug sellers and users is paramount, but police should make a concerted effort to weed out underage participants, too...

An all-night party that ends up in the emergency room or the morgue is hardly a fun, harmless social phenomenon. It's a travesty that can't be tolerated.

THEATRE OF CRUELTY

The cited nightclub, The State Palace Theater, became the subject of a joint federal/New Orleans Police Department (NOPD) operation whose prejudice and ineptitude would be laughable had they not threatened three men who didn't supply drugs with 20 years in jail.

OPERATION RAVE REVIEW

There were no clued-up operatives to investigate the matter, nor appropriate laws to follow it up, so a clueless operative (DEA agent Michael Templeton) and an inappropriate law (the 1986 Title 21, USC Section 856 a.k.a. 'The Crackhouse Law') were used by a grand jury to indict brothers Robert and

Brian Brunet, who managed the State Palace Theater where Kirkland collapsed, and also Donnie Estopinal, who promoted its raves.

This law prohibited maintaining a property 'for the purpose of distributing or using a controlled substance'. It was never intended to apply to owners of nightclubs, but to private landlords allowing crack-cocaine dealers to use their property.

CLUTCHING AT GLOWSTICKS

The law found no evidence to link Brunet, Brunet and Estopinal to drug possession, distribution or manufacturing. Desperation ensued: police cited the common rave fashion accessories (see p44) as tacit acceptance of ecstasy use within the premises: glowsticks apparently brought about the E euphoria and the babies' dummies guarded against jaw convulsions (see p119). If dance promoters for some depraved reason allowed dancing, especially that sort where degenerates touch each other's bodies, they were turning a blind eye to the tactile E culture. (Apparently, in New Orleans people never touch each other unless they've taken ecstasy.) If they went one further and actually distributed water to allay dehydration, they were giving implicit permission to high-level narcotics dealers to ply their trade.

EFFACE FOR THE DEFENCE

The defendants, unsurprisingly, would have none of it. Having developed the State Palace Theater from a dilapidated cinema into a prime rave venue that drew upwards of 4,000 dancers and booked $25,000- (£17,000-) a-time DJs like Paul Oakenfold, the Brunet brothers took umbrage at being likened to sink-estate crack dealers. They reckoned that their venue was friendly, non-violent, welcoming and inclusive, attracting punters that would drive for hours to attend raves.

They maintained that, whilst realising that subcultures do usually involve a motivational drug, they personally tried their damnedest to prevent banned substances being passed on their premises, to the extent of hiring off-duty NOPD cops to help out their own bouncers.

However, after Jillian Kirkland's collapse, media pressure forced the NOPD to pull its cops from the premises – a stupendously counterproductive move. Allegedly, after that the NOPD would not even come to arrest dealers bagged by the club's own security guards.

COUNTRY MANNERS

This seeming misunderstanding of the rave scene by federal agents could well have been compounded by the naivety of the undercover operative Michael Templeton. Formerly a rural police officer, Templeton was dropped in at the deep-end-replete-with-rave-machine of club events involving rollerskating transvestites, fire eaters and trapeze artists. To call it culture shock would suggest something too blasé.

Templeton wanted to find the big fish of the ecstasy world. Unfortunately, all the boys inside the State Palace Theater were veritable minnows - the big fish were overseas in Holland. The minnows would have to suffice.

Although Templeton apprehended several ecstasy dealers over a three-year stint, he didn't arrest any, because of the perceived trivial punishments handed to low-level dealers.

On 9 March 2001, prosecuting lawyers withdrew the charges, apparently because they had offered a deal offering token prison sentences (one or two years as opposed to 20) in return for a guilty plea.

DRIVEL LIBERTIES

However, The American Civil Liberties Union (ACLU) urged the defendants to fight their case. Graham Boyd, head of the ACLU Drug Policy Litigation Project, said: 'Go after the people who deal the drugs, but you can't go after the people who provide the music; and you especially can't go after only the ones who provide a certain kind.'

The Brunet Brothers, in fear of much expensive legal battle, and possibly deterred by the possibility of 20 years in jail if they were to fight the charges and lose, reached (on 17 May 2001) a plea agreement whereby in return for having criminal charges against them dropped they would raise the minimum age of entry to the State Palace Theater to 18. On top of this they would ban overt 'drugs paraphernalia' like glowsticks, pacifiers and masks. Oh, and chillout rooms were out, too. Those places that save lives...no need for them.

Donnie Estopinal, the rave promoter, refused to have anything to do with this and is no longer employed at the State Palace Theater.

FIGHT FOR THE RIGHT TO PARTY

The Electronic Music Defense and Education Fund (EM:DEF), a charity set up, in its own words, 'To raise and provide funds for legal assistance to innocent professionals in the electronic dance music business who are targeted by law enforcement in the expanding campaign against "club drugs"', thought that this set a bad precedent and was determined to fight it:

> *EM:DEF is committed to raising money to challenge the provisions of the settlement. The plea agreement led both* Time Magazine *and* The Times-Picayune *to call the case in New Orleans a failure. After seeking prison time for Robert, Brian, and Donnie, the DEA has settled for a $100,000 [£70,000] fine against a corporation – a fine that was inconsequential compared to the cost of fighting the trial.*
>
> *The case in New Orleans had been on hold for several weeks while prosecutors determined what to do after a refusal to accept a plea by Robert, Brian, and Donnie. The plea and our proposed challenge to the plea will not eliminate the precedent that was set; however, it will prevent law enforcement from banning glowsticks and other items at electronic music events. Private businesses may still ban the items, but public venues will not be allowed to if we win. Furthermore, it will undermine the entire substance of the plead conviction. What will remain painfully clear to anyone evaluating the DEA and their investigation is that they failed to find any wrongdoing on the part of the promoter and management for the club, but bullied a plea agreement anyway to try and save face. There is simply no other interpretation that fits.*
>
> *The case has since been re-opened with the separate charge against each defendant for each and every rave hosted at the State Palace Theater. This could bring an effective punishment of life imprisonment for each man.*

The single-minded measures of McCaffrey may well have led to the incarceration of innocent men like the Brunet brothers, banged up for dogmatic reasons, while the real problem (adulterated MDMA) still walks the streets. McCaffrey, of course, had other ideas.

PANTS ON FIRE

McCaffrey has apparently on occasion been caught being economical - if not downright Spartan - with the truth. The Multidisciplinary Association for Psychedelic Studies (MAPS) - a non-profit drugs research organization - claimed that McCaffrey gave misleading information about what Dr David Smith told him. Smith gathers research on adverse MDMA-related events at the Haight-Ashbury clinic in LA. McCaffrey attributed to him the statement that hundreds of people a month were coming to the clinic seeking treatment for E-related psychosis and severe depression. What Smith in fact said was that there might be hundreds of MDMA-related reports a month submitted to the clinic but, even if there were, the numbers of reports of psychosis and severe depression were a very small minority of them.

CHEER-E-O

On resigning his post on 6 January 2002, McCaffrey said: 'I'm enormously proud of what we've done. We had exploding rates of adolescent drug use, and we've reduced it.'

Many disagree. They reckon that this a definition of 'reduced' that involves an increase of illegal drug use by junior high students of 300 per cent, greater accessibility of drugs, drugs prices at an all-time low and increasing instances of adulterated drugs.

BRITISH BULLSHIT

McCaffrey's reluctant British counterpart, the UK's very own drugs tsar, was Keith Hellawell. His deputy was Michael Trace, former director of the Rehabilitation for Addicted Prisoners' Trust. Hellawell was only reluctant in as much as he hated the tag 'drugs tsar': it sounded too despotic for his approach, and suggested that the problem would be tackled through force alone. In other words, it suited McCaffrey but it didn't suit Hellawell.

FAUX TSAR

The approach of copying the Americans and appointing a 'tsar' was typical of Tony Blair's new 'New Labour' government of 1997. It needed to communicate major policy initiatives, and few things do this better than bold headlines announcing a pseudo-Russian emperor to tackle an area of concern. 'Drugs' was just such an area: the number of new addicts aged under 21 had risen by a third during preceding years, as accordingly had drug-related fatalities. Blair was determined to appoint the right person to address the problem. Nothing but a tsar would do.

Hellawell wasn't just McCaffrey with a British accent; indeed, he initially attracted far less opprobrium from drugs workers than his US counterpart for two main reasons:

- the word 'tsar' as applied to a policy maker sounds inherently ridiculous to the UK sensibility;
- he was the polar opposite of McCaffrey.

YORKSHIRE TERRORIZER

Hellawell was a Yorkshire coalminer. This is significant because Yorkshire coalminers were synonymous with everything that was hard working class and hardline left wing in England. Whether Hellawell himself is a hardline left-winger is doubtful (the fact that he subsequently joined the police force and rose to the position of Chief Constable in West Yorkshire, and later Cleveland, would suggest not) but the connotations are surely there. The Great British Public was less convinced, though.

Unlike McCaffrey, Hellawell seemed a born-again liberal. Like all 'born again' types, he attacked his liberalism with a devoted fervour that would have the old-time free-thinkers looking like Benjamin Disraeli in comparison.

In his early days Hellawell was the typical hard-man copper, never attempting anything so wet as empathizing with suspects – just fixing his ample height and girth inside their personal space and waiting until they were well and truly intimidated. He was very much the 'bad cop' of the two doing the interview – the one who shouts, slams the desk, and offers a cigarette only to pull it way again.

His road to constabulary Damascus happened sometime during the 1960s, when he became what is called by reactionaries a 'heart-bleeding liberal' – someone who tries to understand the motivation behind crime rather than banging up its perpetrators.

Because Hellawell was a hard-arsed Yorkshireman with a difficult childhood and working-class background, he knew first-hand of the link between social deprivation and crime. Even admitting that such a link exists put Hellawell at immediate loggerheads with the type of rightist politician who reckons that ten-hour shifts in a sweat shop at subsistence wages count as gainful employment. Hellawell said: 'I always thought if the root cause of criminal activity was in social deprivation; I wanted to spend money on tackling that, rather than dealing with the consequences. 10 or 15 years ago I was criticized because it was unfashionable, I was set in the role of a radical, having strange ideas. Now it's the way things are going to be done.'

He didn't shirk political blame either: 'Successive Conservative governments stated that the solution to the drug problem lay with the criminal justice system.'

KICK-START BLEEDING LIBERAL

When Hellawell was appointed drugs tsar in 1998, the populist media gleefully lambasted his liberal approach before its Middle England readership. Readers of the *Daily Express*, *Daily Mail* and *Daily Telegraph* had wanted a British McCaffrey, someone who would kick serious druggie butt. Instead they got a seeming 'loony lefty' who symbolically shat on the values their parents fought Hitler for. Hellawell's 'do-gooder' policies had included:

- launching one of the first dedicated drugs squads since the 1960s;
- cautioning cannabis users rather than throwing them in jail to develop a smack habit;
- advocating special drugs courts, which sentenced offenders to addiction clinics rather than jail;
- taking degrees in social policy and law;

- reforming 'outdated' attitudes like the notion that black people are responsible for most crime;
- shutting police-station bars so officers couldn't get pissed after work before being released onto the street;
- speaking out against assaults by prison officers on inmates;
- advocating reform of the law on prostitution and the legalization of brothels;

  and an admittedly bizarre one...
- sending a Christmas card to 'Yorkshire Ripper' Peter Sutcliffe.

BATTERIES NOT INCLUDED

Middle England's denizens feared for their future. They didn't need to, for Tony Blair's New Labour government would eventually see them good. Hellawell was a most unusual type of tsar: he had no real power. For a start he was told that nothing in the 1971 Misuse of Drugs Act was up for negotiation. The most expensive pair of handcuffs couldn't have tied his hands behind his back better than that.

In one respect, and one only, this suited him fine. Strangely for a liberal, Hellawell didn't embrace that emblem of leftist free-thinkers and rightist libertarians alike – legalization of drugs. While Hellawell believed that jail was unsuitable for those convicted of possession of soft drugs, he maintained that no listed drug – not even cannabis – should be legalized or decriminalized. He said: 'The debate on decriminalization has gone on for some time. I'm happy for the debate to go on, but it needs to be informed... All that I have seen over the years about that debate has led me to believe that decriminalization or legalization would not help.' In a way this is hardly surprising – he was an ex-copper, after all.

JACK STRAW MAN

Hellawell was really just a Blair-constructed straw man to be burned down at a later date. For a start, initially he had no budget of his own. He personally was paid £103,000 ($149,000) per year, but he had no money allotted to institute reform. He could draw up a strategy, but he couldn't pay for its implementation.

Michael Trace later explained that, despite the lack of budget, the initial six months were a success, because at that stage Hellawell and he were carrying on an open-minded consultation period with experts in the field, looking at preventative and educational measures rather than law enforcement. Meanwhile, his (and Tony Blair's) press secretary Alastair Campbell were emphasizing New Labour's 'hard on drugs' public stance, backed up by cabinet ministers giving major speeches to that effect. Behind the scenes, though, they were happy to let Hellawell and Trace continue with their 'softly softly' approach.

Ann Taylor, chair of the Cabinet subcommittee on drugs, outlined three key objectives for this strategy on the cheap: to reduce

- drug supply;
- health risks;
- demand amongst young people.

The basis for this grand plan in tackling drugs was to make educators, social workers, police forces, law enforcers, magistrates, medics and rehabilitators work together.

In this much, Hellawell was like McCaffrey – he favoured a regional approach, with local media campaigns aimed at young people, including leaflets, posters and interactive websites.

REGIONAL DISSEMBLY

This involved local authorities appointing their own anti-drugs coordinators, one step down the ladder from Hellawell, and taking on (to combine the Russian motif with a delicatessen counter) 'mini-tsar' posts. Hellawell said: 'I am convinced that the commitment, co-operation and willingness to work together at a national and local level will help to create a healthier and safer society.'

Peter Rigby of the London Drug Policy Forum was impressed. He reckoned new plans would end a 'mishmash' of agencies responsible for tackling drugs: 'We welcome the government's recognition of the crucial role of local authorities in delivering anti-drugs strategies.'

TSAR WARS

Hellawell favoured a more generic and integrated approach to drugs education, believing that peer education worked better than the didactic approach because, even if it didn't prevent experimentation, it may prevent the transition to Class A drugs.

Hellawell instigated a revised school curriculum with new guidelines on teaching drug education, where community police officers would support teachers.

MONEY TO CHURN

In 1999, Tony Blair decided to bung his drugs dealer a quid or two after it emerged that the free approach had singularly failed to work. Together they set out a ten-year strategy to break the link between drugs and crime, and £250 million ($360 million) was allotted over three years to achieve this. Blair told Parliament:

> *There is no more serious problem than the link between crime and drugs. Already the Government has introduced minimum sentences for drug dealers of seven years, mandatory drug testing, new drug treatment orders and an extra £220m [$320 million] for a strategy to fight drugs. The drug menace is one we are determined to fight at every single level, through tougher measures in the law, better provision in the courts, better education in our schools and better treatment for drug offenders.*

FALLOUT KELTER

That's was when Hellawell and Trace fell apart. They continued working together amicably enough, but Hellawell lost a lot of his radical liberalism, while Trace veered toward advocating the decriminalization of soft drugs.

Hellawell began towing a 'drugs are bad' party line and also borrowing mannerisms from McCaffrey and adapting them to the British sensibility - his equivalent of McCaffrey's 'bracelet' interviews being homilies to halcyon days when girls played hopscotch in the street and boys' boredom threshold wasn't lowered by crack cocaine and computer gaming.

MO-GO AREA

At this time Mo Mowlam – probably the only member of Blair's cabinet that the British public in any way liked – was appointed the new minister in charge of the Cabinet Office's drug coordination unit. Her approach was far more liberal than those of her colleagues (indeed she confessed to smoking cannabis during her student days – and unlike Clinton she inhaled until her lungs nearly burst) and favoured 'radical' measures such as the legalization of cannabis for medical use. This put her at immediate loggerheads with Home Secretary Jack Straw and the Health Secretary Alan Milburn.

A report by the International Narcotics Control Board (INCB), entitled *Globalization And New Technologies*, states that drug traders are discovering ever more sophisticated ways to use the Internet to sell ecstasy.

When a Police Foundation report on drugs law reform called for less restrictive cannabis and ecstasy laws, Straw – knowing that Mowlam would be sympathetic to its recommendations, and with the backing of Tony Blair – pulled rank and rebutted the report without allowing her a say in the matter. Mike Trace, in a January 2002 interview with the *Guardian*, revealed that the Prime Minister had told Mowlam that she may indeed be right in her views, but that was of lesser importance than his government being seen as a 'soft touch' before the media. In any case, Blair himself agreed with Straw.

Mowlam got her unit to respond to the report by drawing up a fully costed breakdown of drugs laws and tax called 'Nuclear Option'. Again, Straw overruled her and bucked the issue by getting civil servants to draw up a paper exploring slightly laxer policing of cannabis (this has since come into force).

RIGHTI-NO

David Floyd, writing in the socialist *Chartist Magazine*, gave his opinion that rightist opinion was all too influential upon this ostensibly centrist government:

> *Sadly though, the Tories are a factor in the current state of the debate on drug policy. This involves a quaint coalition of Liberal*

Democrats and columnists from the Independent On Sunday *[UK newspaper with no political allegiance] delivering sensible arguments against prohibition, pitched against tabloid front pages screaming 'ecstasy killed my daughter', while [Home Secretary] Jack Straw cowers under the table in his office with his hands over his ears. It's not much of a contest.*

THAT SAYS IT ALL

The catchphrases adopted by the new campaign were the atrocious 'People Power' (reminiscent of 1970s BBC situation comedy *Citizen Smith*), and the kneecap-threatening 'Rat On A Rat', which encouraged citizens to attract violent retribution by grassing up drug dealers for the greater good of all.

Although the ten-year plan to tackle drug abuse had targets to cut consumption of heroin, cocaine and other drugs, no baseline figures were published, which made it impossible to judge if the targets were being met. In other words: it was of bugger all use.

The ten-year 'strategy' included:

- a minimum sentence of seven years' imprisonment for those convicted of a third offence of supplying Class A drugs like ecstasy;
- an extension of drug testing to identify offenders committing crime to buy drugs;
- piloting of Drug Treatment and Testing Orders forcing offenders to take detoxification treatment;
- a £20 million ($29 million) joint initiative with the police to accelerate the development of arrest referral schemes;
- rigorous enforcement of community sentences for people convicted of crimes such as shoplifting that fed their drug habit.

AS EVERY SCHOOLBOY DOESN'T YET KNOW

The Healthy Schools Standard, launched in October 1999, was partly implemented through every UK teacher's 'second subject': Personal, Social and Health Education (PSHE). Inside schools, it comprised:

- providing information about local drug scenes and helping schools to develop programmes responsive to pupil needs and the local situation;
- establishing pilot projects to encourage links between care groups and their local schools;
- health professionals supporting teachers in the delivery of drug prevention education;
- projects covering related information like smoking, alcohol and sexual health;
- a National School Drug Safety Team to provide schools with up-to-date advice on drug education.

Outside schools, it comprised:

- drug prevention projects, targeted at young people at particular risk of drug misuse, commissioned by 11 'Health Action Zones' in the UK, covering truants and school excludees, young offenders, young homeless people and children of drug-misusing parents;
- the government working with Sport England (the brand name of the English Sports Council) and the Youth Justice Board (a non-departmental public body) to set up a range of projects under the Positive Futures initiative, aiming to divert vulnerable young people aged 10–16 years into sport and healthy activities and away from drug misuse and antisocial activity;
- the National Drugs Telephone Helpline run by Healthwise (a Liverpool-based health information service) under contract to the Department of Health to distribute health promotion materials free of charge;
- the Resource-Net Internet service, funded by the Department of Health, to enable teachers, parents, voluntary groups and other interested parties easy access to drug prevention materials;
- LOCATE, an Internet-based database of community activities for drug education and prevention.

TOO LITTLE, TOO LATE

Anti-drugs campaigners weren't impressed. This is not surprising, as being unimpressed is basically their job.

Using an acronym that sounds like a cheap Czech car is perhaps unwise for a pressure group, but that's exactly what the Standing Conference on Drug Abuse (SCODA) did. SCODA didn't like Hellawell's attitude, which – while being a bit more hardline than before – was still slanted toward prevention and education rather than inflicting torture on drug dealers. Its objections were that of the £1.4 billion ($2 billion) allocated towards fighting drugs in 1997–98:

- 62 per cent went on enforcement;
- 13 per cent went on treatment;
- 12 per cent went on prevention and education;
- 13 per cent went in tackling international supply.

This balance would, according to the latest announcements, alter to:

- 61 per cent on enforcement;
- 32 per cent on treatment;
- 5 per cent on tackling supplies;
- 1.5 per cent on prevention and education.

SCODA chief executive Roger Howard said: 'Those working in drug education and prevention programmes would, I suspect, have also expected to see a more significant shift in resources to reflect the government's commitment to helping prevent drug problems ever arising.'

LEFT-WINGER NOT KNOWING WHAT THE RIGHT-WINGER IS DOING

This report by Jay Rayner, from the *Guardian* newspaper's website, indicates the in-house turmoil within which Hellawell was find some semblance of sanity in early 2000:

> *It was meant to be a good news day, a way for Britain's drug tsar to reclaim the political agenda from what he has come to call, with increasing disdain, 'the spin machine'. Sadly for Keith Hellawell, the spin machine had not yet finished its cycle.*

Before an audience of 100 teachers and drug workers in a motel on the outskirts of Gloucester last week, the former Chief Constable of West Yorkshire announced the recruitment of 680 new drug workers. '£500,000 [$700,000] of government money has been put aside for the recruitment drive,' Hellawell said. 'And training will be given. I can't say yet what form the training will take, but it will be paid for out of the seized asset fund.'

He said the same announcement was being made simultaneously by Cabinet Office Minister Mo Mowlam, to whom he reports. At that moment Mowlam was appearing on BBC Radio 4's Woman's Hour, *but she seemed to have other things on her mind. While passing reference to the recruitment drive was made, she used the broadcast instead for something more pungent: an attack on elements in Whitehall which, she said, 'were trying to put the knife in' by briefing journalists that her brain tumour illness had left her unable to do her job.*

Mowlam's assault on her detractors was widely reported the next day. The announcement about the recruitment of new drug workers was ignored.

Once again Hellawell had seen significant progress in his war on drugs obscured by fallout from the Whitehall spin machine. Mowlam is well known to be less than fond of Hellawell, whom she is said to regard as being 'too Chief Constable'. She has more time for his deputy, Mike Trace, who comes from the world of field work with addicts. But Hellawell is more likely to see it simply as part of a growing problem he has in getting his message across. He has been derided for allegedly suggesting that the Government should consider buying Afghanistan's entire opium crop to stop it getting on to the streets as heroin.

He has been lambasted for apparently suggesting the Internet is encouraging drug use among young people and criticized for failings in pilot drug treatment schemes he has introduced.

He will also know that the support he has expressed in today's Observer *for the 'depenalization' of the possession of cannabis – a recommendation of a forthcoming report by the Police Foundation – will prove controversial.*

He is irritated by the way he is portrayed in the media. 'I do get cross when I read about what I have or haven't done, said or haven't said,' he said. 'The spin machine looks like it's trying to pin a tail on the donkey with its eyes shut. They've found me and decided I'm going to be the target of derision.'

Yet he still does not feel he can afford to ignore the hacks. In Gloucester he spent 20 minutes talking to the drug workers who had travelled from all over the country for a conference on drug use among young people with special needs. But he gave the smattering of journalists present almost two hours.

'We're actually doing everything we said we would do and doing it on time,' he told them. 'People from other countries have seen what we're doing in Britain and they say they don't understand the stick I'm getting. At the United Nations congress on drug use in 1998 I was given a full session to present our programme to 190 nations. Even General Barry McCaffrey, who's heading up the American drug programme, was surprised at the speed with which we've got everything going.'

He launches into a list of successes: the reduction in criminality among offenders who have been part of referral schemes for treatment, the introduction of drug-free wings in some prisons, the small reductions that have been seen in the numbers of people saying they have ever tried drugs. But mostly he wants to talk about the turnaround in official attitudes to the problem of drugs.

'Successive Conservative governments stated that the solution to the drug problem lay with the criminal justice system,' he said. 'Now funds are being shifted into treatment and education.' Hence the need for 680 new drug workers: the agencies implementing drug treatment and education policy have the money to do the job, he said, they just don't have the bodies to do it. Now that problem would be solved.

He has, he says, managed to get more than £250 million [$360 million] of new money out of the Treasury to fight his war. His list of achievements is indeed impressive, but there are still problems. More than 50 per cent of offenders issued with Drug Treatment and Testing Orders, one of Hellawell's pet projects, piloted in three areas so far, have returned to using drugs.

'Yes,' he says, 'but the general level of criminality and drug spending among them has dropped.'

There are also increases in the use of cocaine. This, he admits, is a cause for grave concern. 'In the last British Crime Survey covering 1996–8 we saw an increase of cocaine use from 1 per cent to 3 per cent among the 15–29 age group, mostly around the club scene in London, Liverpool and Nottingham. This is a threefold increase.

'In the next two years we are going to see a further increase. It's becoming cheaper and more socially acceptable. Clearly this is bad news for someone like me in this job.' But, he insists, the important issue is to look at drug policy as a whole.

'What I have done is lift the stone on the hidden truth about drugs in Britain, which is that we need to discriminate between different drugs and the relative harm caused and then talk openly about the difference we can make. The focus is going to be on the drugs that cause the major harm.'

This means accepting that cannabis use – and even the recreational use of ecstasy and amphetamines – is a low priority and that resources should instead be concentrated on narcotics such as like heroin and cocaine.

The problem is that to talk of such things is seen by Labour to be politically dangerous, hence the ridiculing of Clare Short when she said it might be worth considering decriminalising marijuana and the backlash Mowlam experienced when she admitted having inhaled... Sources have suggested former Cabinet Officer Minster Jack Cunningham was responsible for most of it.

Sometimes Hellawell says it is simply the media misrepresenting him. He says the story about buying the Afghan crop of opium is a case in point. 'The issue did arise. I simply asked whether there is any logic to the fact that the opium crop in some countries is licensed and legal, because it is used to produce diamorphine for medicinal purposes, and illegal in others. I just said we might look at this question.'

Hellawell loves talking about studies and reports, to prove how well he is doing. The journalists in Gloucester who had come to report his visit were less than interested.

They wanted to know whether he was going to recommend giving more powers to local police so they could lock up the drug dealers crowding the city's streets. These are the questions the public ask. Near the city centre, where the Starbucks coffee shops and the cosy bookshops and boutiques give way to the clutter of inner-city decay, is the Vauxhall Inn in Barton Street. Two months ago the brewery put in a new landlord because of the drug dealing that was rife in and about the pub.

The windows are now obscured by signs promising immediate police action against anybody found dealing or taking drugs on the premises. The pub itself has improved remarkably, but the problem itself still exists.

Around the corner are modern public lavatories which Joe Lynch, the new landlord, says should never have been built. 'It's a constant menace,' he says. 'That is the biggest place for taking and receiving.'

Inside, is a yellow plastic box fixed on the wall by the council for used needles. A general election is expected within 18 months. New Labour will then seek a second term in government based on its record.

On the doorsteps of Barton Street the small print of Hellawell's successes is unlikely to be as attractive to the electorate as the headlines politicians like to use. And the drug tsar knows it.

FARE HELLAWELL

The Blair government finally applied the torches to straw man Keith Hellawell, and with it the position of 'drugs tsar', in August 2001. In truth, the kindling had been laid for some time.

After Hellawell's departure, the new Home Secretary David Blunkett took over responsibility for coordinating national policy, and the position of 'drugs tsar' became redundant. He said: 'I have not had an opportunity to discuss with [Hellawell] what role he might play in the future. I want to look at that as part of what we do in the whole area of drugs policy. I have got to talk to him and mark out what the best way forward will be.'

His future role turned out to be that of token part-time adviser, with sod-all responsibility.

Almost from the moment of his inception, Hellawell had stood politically between an especially crystalline rock and the hardest of hard places. And this was just within the New Labour cabinet. Trace said: 'It had become clear to us that having outsiders like us trying to run the show was not going very well. In my view, the civil service refused to work for us. It was obvious by the time the [May 2001 General] Election was coming up that having outsiders with no direct powers, overseeing the implementation of a complex interdepartmental programme, was not working.'

SOCCER PUNCH

It's not over till the dour Scotsman speaks. An initiative announcement of 9 April 2001 told the tsar he was no longer wanted more effectively than any dismissal notice: Hellawell was replaced on the platform by Manchester United manager (and New Labour funder) Sir Alex Ferguson.

This initiative included, in the words of the 10 Downing Street website, 'A £300 million [$435 million] boost to tackle the evil of drugs in Britain and to mobilize communities against drugs' that comprised:

- £220 million [$320 million] over three years for police and local communities in England and Wales to disrupt local drug markets and drug-related crime;
- £15 million [$22 million] over three years to help Drug Action Teams work effectively in their local communities;
- £5 milliion [$7 million] over two years to increase the involvement of sports stars as role models and develop Positive Futures, a scheme to steer young people away from drug misuse through sport;

- £50 million [$70 million] to accelerate the drug testing programme within the criminal justice scheme.

Chancellor Gordon Brown said: 'Today's initiative starts from the only place where the fight against drugs can be won, in our communities. It is a fight that cannot be won by Government alone, by legislation alone or even by cash alone – to win the fight against drugs we must dig deeper into the very core of our communities, giving power to community organizations and drawing strength from each other as we organize against the dealer and the pusher.'

Of course, what that day's initiative categorically did not start with was the man ostensibly in charge of starting it: the drugs tsar. The tsar-free strategies included:

- high-visibility policing of drug hot spots;
- increase in neighbourhood wardens;
- support to parents and residents groups;
- improved security including CCTV and street lighting;
- extra truancy sweeps.

And, of course, kicking a ball around a field and tackling from behind. Alex Ferguson droned: 'I am giving my full support to Communities Against Drugs and to Positive Futures in particular. Drugs ruin the potential of too many of our children and sport provides a valuable alternative to the dangerous diversion they can create.' Hellawell may well have become a City supporter after that.

CRUMBLING EDIFICE

Mike Trace summed up Hellawell's emperorship as that of a man who began with a genuine commitment to action, but was gradually seduced by the spin-doctoring influence of his employers. He said: 'In the first year [Hellawell] worked like a dog and was committed to what he was trying to achieve; I think that was a great time for him. As time passed, I think he became disengaged from the hard slog of implementation, concentrating on appearances only. It is a shame because there is more to him than that. In the last year he attracted a lot of criticism. The drug strategy we developed contained some crucial programmes that need to be followed through. It would be disappointing if this work – reducing drug-related crime, health problems and social exclusion – loses momentum under the new arrangements.'

THE PRO-E STANCE

> *'As one of the 200,000 "feared" to be taking illegal drugs, ie ecstasy, this New Year's Eve, and having done so every year for many years now, may I ask what it is the government is fearful of?*
>
> *'Ecstasy is not a dangerous drug and there will be many people proving this on New Year's Eve. The casualty wards meanwhile will be full of alcohol-related cases.'* – Anonymous correspondent to the *Guardian* newspaper, 28 December 2001

The problem with hysteria is that it uses the 'commonsense' argument, wielded by those deficient in reasoning skills, to pummel the feeblest of contrary opinion into pinko commie mush. For example, when in April 1996 Mary Hartnoll (a senior social worker working in Glasgow) had the temerity to point out that scaremongering about ecstasy was contrary to youngsters' experience, and that ecstasy was a 'relatively safe drug', the usual suspects lined up to offer their worthless opinions:

- Paul Betts: 'To come from such a prominent person, it's absolutely stupid. She should get her facts right. American research has found that ecstasy causes permanent and irreversible brain damage. If she wants to promote that, she's a silly woman.'
- Tory MP Nigel Evans: 'There must be many youngsters living a hell of an existence who would like to meet Mary Hartnoll so that she can see what impact this so-called relatively safe drug means to those who do not instantly die.'
- Councillor James Coleman, chairman of Glasgow's licensing board: 'I don't know where Miss Hartnoll gets this information. We believe that

the majority of young people don't take drugs and her type of message sends out the wrong signal.'

- A Scottish Office (of the then Tory government) spokesman: 'There is no such thing as a risk-free drug. The misuse of any drug can cause serious harm or lasting damage and even death. It would be quite wrong to send a false message to society, especially the young, that drugs are not harmful.'

That is only the fate awaiting those who only suggest ecstasy 'isn't as dangerous as it's made out to be'. Those who go one further and actually promote the cause of ecstasy have a particularly hard time of it.

SHIT STORY, SHIT-STIRRER

In January 1997, Brian Harvey, lead singer of UK teen band East 17, gave a notorious interview. Any pearls of musical wisdom gleaned from this *tête-à-tête* are long since forgotten, but the peripheral matter of ecstasy use decidedly isn't. He dropped a few ecstatic bollocks during this interview, and no mistake.

- He said that ecstasy can make you a better person.
- He boasted that he had taken 12 Es at once with no ill effects.
- He further boasted that he had driven a car on E and remained totally in control of the vehicle.

This was music to the ears of then Prime Minister, John Major, who would have to call a general election within the year, and whose Conservative Party's popularity was currently crawling around at seabed level. Not only did he mention it in Parliament, but he incited Tory MPs to demand Harvey's arrest on the charge of incitement to break the law.

Harvey was duly sacked from East 17, though too late because the combo's records were already banned by 17 UK radio stations. Furthermore, five pages of the *Daily Mirror*, a populist UK tabloid, were devoted to recycling old news about dangers of E. These were bordered by pictures of young angels apparently 'killed' by the drug.

Had Harvey stuck with the 'ecstasy is good for you' line without moving onto his multiple-pill-popping and car-driving bravado, he may have raised a contentious but valid debating point. As it was, he wasted his opportunity by breeding hysteria. On 19 April 2002, the *Daily Mirror* reported that Harvey had never rebuilt his career after that interview and was now filing for bankruptcy. It concluded:

> *The R&B artist [Brian Harvey] has been jinxed since being sacked from East 17 for taking the drug ecstasy. Last year he was severely attacked by machete-wielding thugs outside a nightclub in Nottingham. And to make matters worse, his new singing career has bombed despite costly marketing campaigns.*
>
> *A source said, 'Brian is very depressed. His luck has run out. He's penniless and, ironically, is living in Walthamstow E17. He really wants people to stand up and listen to his new music but no one is interested in him anymore. Filing for bankruptcy is the final straw for him.'*

JASON LIVES

Other supporters of MDMA are more considered in their approach, though decidedly less prominent.

'Jason', a mid-20s graduate from northeast England, is nearly always stoned on E. Quite what the point of that is, is anybody's guess (it's generally acknowledged that you need the lows to appreciate the highs) but it seems to work for him. He believes that E-taking is rife among professionals and a good thing too. Quoted in the *Newcastle Journal*, he said: 'It is extremely common – people just do not realize. The whole thing about drugs has been demonized unfairly. Those who have first-hand experience know they are not half as dangerous as they are meant to be.'

SENSIBLE LIMITS

Students for Sensible Drug Policy (SSDP) is a student organization that, in its opinion, aims to deliver the true facts about drugs legislation. A publicity document reads: 'We are the generation the drug laws were supposed to protect. It's up to us to stand up and say, this isn't working.'

Beyond the above arguments, SSDP argues that in practice drugs prohibition is discriminatory, with the rules being more stringently applied against poorer communities, with wealthier people being able to afford better lawyers (this is true throughout the legal system) and ethnic peoples.

WASTE OF PRISON RESOURCES

Many argue that prison is best reserved for violent criminals who are a genuine threat to society, and yet almost a quarter of the two million Americans in jail are there for non-violent drug offences, many of them parents.

Ecstasy seizures worldwide in 2001 accounted for 25 million pills, at a street value of approximately £400 million ($580 million). The largest numbers were uncovered in the UK, followed by Germany and the USA. *Guardian*, 31 May 2002

Nora Callahan, director of the November Coalition, a pressure group for 'so-called' drug-war prisoners, cites over a million 'drug war orphans' in America and asserts that they are more than five times as likely as other kids to end up behind bars themselves. She writes: 'Our relentless and punitive prosecution of the drug war against adults, and the subsequent explosion in our prison population has had dire consequences for children as well.'

HYPERBOLLOCKS

Supporters of MDMA believe that media coverage of fatalities and long-term brain damage is wildly exaggerated. They argue that animal experiments have no relevance to humans and indeed condemn the butchering of monkeys for information that is, in their opinion, of no proven use. They claim that the problem of serotonin depletion has been known for years and can be remedied by taking an antidepressant like Prozac or – for those of an herbalist bent – St John's Wort.

RIGHT ON GEEZER

It isn't only the left side that promotes the cause of ecstasy. This report comes from the libertarian right of Conservative (the capital C is important) thinking, which cites FA Hayek's 1944 anti-corporatist tract

The Road To Serfdom as its bible. Nicholas Saunders writes (I have abridged this):

> *Imagine a regime so totalitarian that it will not allow its young citizens to dance when they want. Imagine that this regime introduced a law which banned dance parties unless they were authorized by the State...*
>
> *In order to combat the subversive profiteering free-market dance party entrepreneurs the state would form Lifestyle Police. Using undercover agents they would infiltrate the parties...and try to prevent them going ahead, by turning away thousands of dissident party-goers and arresting the organizers.*
>
> *This is truly a regime of which Stalin or Hitler himself would be proud, implementing socialist policies to protect the citizens from their own moral weakness.*
>
> *Sadly the above is not a fantasy, it is based on reality. In Britain in 1990 all this happened, not under a Communist regime, but under an increasingly authoritarian Conservative government. What the tabloid press called the acid house party generated a momentum for yet more restrictions on our civil liberties.*
>
> *This is another example of the Lifestyle Police in action, but the Lifestyle Police are not the police in uniform, they are the conservative, intolerant bigots who demand uniformity...They truly believe that they represent decent values when in fact they have narrow intolerant values... [UK moral campaigner the late] Mary Whitehouse is the Lifestyle Policewoman par excellence.*
>
> *The Lifestyle Police are controlled by members of a powerful but little known clandestine entryist political party known as the Safety Nazis. They are politically active in the Conservative Party and the Green Party. In America the Safety Nazis' greatest political success was the Prohibition Act. Only the valiant actions of the Mafia managed to save America by machine gunning leading Safety Nazis.*
>
> *Safety Nazis want to ban things: video nasties, cigarettes, drink, drugs, loud music, pornography, toy guns, real guns, artificial*

additives, swear words on TV, fast cars, unusual sexual practices, dancing around Stonehenge on the solstice and acid house parties. They also make you do things for your own good, like wear a seat belt and watch public information films...

Safety Nazis have a secret greeting: Sieg Health...

The difference between the Lifestyle Police and the Safety Nazis is one of degree. Safety Nazis are politically motivated...

The Lifestyle Police and their allies the Safety Nazis do not like people enjoying themselves. Why else would they introduce a law to stop people dancing all night?

Britain's archaic licensing laws demand that public entertainments such as nightclubs must be licensed...to serve drink, to play music and to allow dancing. Why do you need a licence? Because the Safety Nazis want to make sure that you're safe... In effect there is a state enforced curfew, strictly monitored by the Lifestyle Police. Break the curfew and you lose your licence, putting you out of business.

I have been to nightclubs in pre-perestroika Moscow that were open all hours. I know of nowhere else in the world – except Ireland – that has more restrictive licensing laws, and in Ireland nobody pays the law any attention...

The police and the authorities became tired of being outwitted and resorted to roadblocks, bugging phones, harassing organizers and mass detentions... [The] tabloid newspapers waged an hysterical scare campaign, branding party organizers as evil drug pushers who were poisoning Britain's youth... [Pirate] (i.e. free market) radio stations which broadcast party location information were raided and shut down... Civil liberties were crushed in order to stop young people committing the heinous crime of dancing all night without a licence. The Safety Nazis advanced another step on their long march.

Late last year Dr. Timothy Leary, the guru of psychedelia, was refused entry into Britain... The Home Office refused him entry, but where were the human rights activists protesting about restrictions on freedom of speech?... Timothy Leary is an interesting man with interesting ideas, yet I am not allowed to hear what he has to say. The Lifestyle Police strike again.

THE ALEXANDER TECHNIQUE

Both extremes of the debate are wrong, as is every shade of opinion between them. When scientists still can't agree whether cannabis - a drug that has been around for several *millennia* - is carcinogenic, it is no surprise that the mere 90-year-old MDMA is a near-total enigma to them. Spokespeople on ecstasy tend to preach a version of the curate's egg: they are *right in parts*. It is up to the prospective ecstasy user, or the concerned parent, to decide for themselves which particular parts are right and act accordingly.

I end by paraphrasing Alexander Shulgin. He's the most knowledgeable bloke around.

BE INFORMED

- Ecstasy does not kill, although attendant circumstances sometimes do.
- Excessive non-stop dancing turns you into an odorous, scabrous parody of humanity.

BE UNINFORMED

- Ecstasy may or may not cause long-term brain damage in humans - no one knows.

Now choose...

ADDITIONAL INFO

FURTHER READING

IN PRINT

- Shulgin, Alexander and Shulgin, Ann: *PiHKAL: A Chemical Love Story* (Transform Press, 1991)
- Holland, Julie (editor): *Ecstasy – The Complete Guide: A Comprehensive Look At The Risks And Benefits Of MDMA* (Park Street Press, 2001)

ONLINE

- **www.drugscope.co.uk** – website of the UK's foremost drugs charity. Objective, bang up to date and essential
- **www.ecstasy.org** – open-minded ecstasy resource, though it does border on pro-E propaganda; comprehensive and informative nonetheless
- **www.theantidrug.com** – the 'Anti Drug' was the brand name for General Barry McCaffrey's 'Yeah paranoia, nay pills' campaign. This is its self-explanatory website
- **www.freevibe.com** – www.theantidrug.com's sister site, intended for 'yoof' paranoiacs, is a teen magazine slanted toward drugs
- **www.clubbed.com** – the rave must-have. Provides all manner of facilities from searching for local parties to checking on current instances of adulterated drugs
- **alt.drugs.ecstasy** – the main rollers' Internet newsgroup. Lurk here to catch the rave dialect diamond in the rough, or even abandon that Caps Lock key and have some crack with the ravers

INDEX